Vegetable Growing

Vegetable Growing

Growing

A Money-Saving Guide

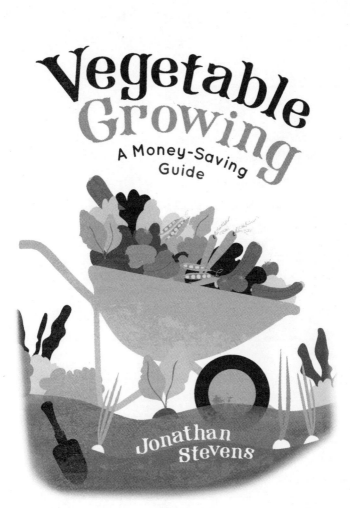

Jonathan Stevens

Michael O'Mara Books Limited

For my wife and my boys

First published in Great Britain in 2017 by
Michael O'Mara Books Limited
9 Lion Yard
Tremadoc Road
London SW4 7NQ

A CIP catalogue record for this book is available from the British
Library.

Papers used by Michael O'Mara Books Limited are natural, recyclable
products made from wood grown in sustainable forests. The
manufacturing processes conform to the environmental regulations of
the country of origin.

ISBN: 978-1-78243-763-5 in paperback print format
ISBN: 978-1-78243-855-7 in ebook format

1 2 3 4 5 6 7 8 9 10

Designed and typeset by K.DESIGN, Winscombe, Somerset
Illustrations by Andrew Pinder
Printed and bound by CPI Group (UK) Ltd, Croydon CR0 4YY

www.mombooks.com

Contents

Acknowledgements

Thanks to all at Michael O'Mara Books for giving me the opportunity to write *Vegetable Growing*.

To my lovely wife Ailsa for all her support while I shirked parenting responsibilities to sit in a room and write.

To my friends and fellow plot holders at the Burnham-on-Crouch allotments for all their tried-and-tested tips and tricks, so many of which appear in this book.

A massive thank you to all the people who have taken the time to visit my blog, Real Men Sow, over the past few years. As always, thanks for reading.

And a million thank yous to my wonderful mum, for her patience, endless enthusiasm and teaching me the way of the soil.

Introduction

Ah, ten years ago …

There I was, twenty-four years old, not long out of university and still the proud owner of a full head of hair. My gardening-mad mother, Jan, was undergoing treatment for cancer and was becoming increasingly frustrated at not being able to get outside and dig. So one chilly afternoon my brother and I helped her make a couple of raised beds to grow some vegetables.

Although Mum has always loved gardening, growing vegetables was new for her, and gave her something fresh to focus on while her treatment continued. We spent evenings looking at books and seed catalogues, and I became mildly obsessed with the *River Cottage* TV programmes. The summer came, and together we spent time growing vegetables and, thankfully, Mum kicked cancer's butt.

I realized a few things during this time: cancer is rubbish, mums are incredibly important and we should always be nice to them, and growing vegetables for your dinner is absolutely the most satisfying, glorious hobby.

The following year, Mum and I took on a redundant allotment plot together. Three years later, Mum stopped watching over my shoulder, and I figured I must be doing something right. A steady stream of incredibly tasty fruit and veg continued to wing its way to my kitchen and soon I was spending most weekends and plenty of summer evenings at the plot. I'd found there was something joyful about allotments, growing your own food and living within the seasons, and I longed to tell the world about this new discovery. However, I found the fussiness of cauliflowers and just how much better homegrown tomatoes taste tricky subjects to shoehorn into conversation. My football team weren't overly interested, and my mates humoured me for a minute or so before moving on to more suitable pub discussions – nothing to do with allotments.

So, like you do these days, I set up a social media account and found a hashtag. Suddenly, everything changed, and at the click of a button I was exposed to hundreds of people who loved growing vegetables! Some even enjoyed discussing cauliflowers, and some even went as far as writing about their escapades on allotments. I began reading blogs and my evenings were spent working through the feed on my blog reader rather than watching the TV.

I realized that, despite my initial difficulty finding people to talk to, allotments were becoming popular again and I'd just been looking in the wrong place. Lots of people were discovering the wonders of growing your own food and, like me, many were newcomers. We talked on Twitter and passed on tips to each other, and as I watched these useful nuggets of information gradually disappear down my feed, I developed an urge to try and save them. I wanted to collect all the great advice I'd picked up from the internet and fellow plot holders, and put it all in one place, while also celebrating the marvellous, life-affirming qualities of growing your own food. I wanted to help people and I wanted to show my absolute happiness at being an allotment holder, so I bought some webspace and Real Men Sow, the 'cheery allotment blog', was born.

At the same time, I embarked on a mission to find out how much I could save by growing my own fruit and vegetables on a half-sized allotment plot. By this time, I'd moved into my own place and had become intrigued by the cost of food in the shops and concerned about the cash in my pocket. I began weighing my harvests and comparing the weight to equivalent supermarket prices.

I made a spreadsheet to calculate savings, and weighed every fruit and veg harvest for twelve months, from leafy salads to bumper butternut squashes. My lovely girlfriend thought I was nuts, but hey, I'm a man, we do these odd projects. She's now my wife, so I guess it didn't put her off too much.

My calculations told me that I saved approximately £500 growing my own fruit and veg that year. I found the project strangely fun, so ever since I've geared my allotment and veg patches towards maximum productivity and focused on those fruit and veg that I now know save me and my new family the most money.

I wrote up my monthly findings on Real Men Sow, and to my surprise, a few people started following the blog. By the end of the year, a few more were following, some had downloaded my sample spreadsheet, and I'd even been mentioned briefly in a gardening magazine. I checked my web stats and a fair chunk of people had taken the time to visit and read a few pages of Real Men Sow over the past twelve months. I asked my mum if it was her repeatedly pressing F5, but she denied this. To my amazement, I had readers …

Since then, Real Men Sow has been featured in national newspapers, magazines and on TV, and now receives over 100,000 visits a year. My blog's popularity still surprises me, but it is lovely to know that people are reading what I'm putting up. This book is the culmination of seven years of blogging, and focuses on frugal allotmenteering, including planning your plot, looking after the plants and practical tips for keeping your costs down, such as clever ways of making freebie alternatives to common growing tools.

There is also a section offering advice on which fruit and veg will save you the most money, as well as a guide on the key seasonal jobs for spring, summer, autumn and winter. The book is aimed at beginners and improvers alike, and is designed to offer uncomplicated advice on cultivating reliable and satisfying crops that not only save you money, but build veg-growing confidence, too.

For me, there is no more important year in allotment growing than the first one. The first year shapes your veg future, changes eating habits and, most importantly, decides whether you're even going to like allotmenteering at all. So getting off to a good start in allotment life is vital, and that's something else I'm hoping the book realizes: to help beginners achieve a fruitful first year, rather than hanging up tools at the end of the summer because all that grew were weeds.

When I started out, I was lucky to have my mother. As I have said, she is a passionate, lifelong gardener, and at the beginning she watched over me, lending a helping hand whenever I needed it. She made my first year a success, and if it wasn't for her, I'd not be loving my allotment the way I do today.

I hope this book goes some way towards helping you enjoy a productive first year – a year that lives long in the memory as the springboard to many more wonderful days on your allotment plot, and saves you a few quid in the process.

CHAPTER 1

Getting Started

So, You're Thinking of Making That Call to the Local Allotment Committee ...

I remember making my call. I'd just moved to a little riverside town in Essex called Burnham-on-Crouch. It was 2007, and I'd been inspired by the original *River Cottage* series, which I thought was absolutely the best thing I'd ever seen on telly.

Declaring my intentions to my sceptical then-girlfriend-now-wife Ailsa, I took myself off for a sneaky walk around the allotments. I'm not afraid to admit that the experience was all rather intoxicating. Spring was upon us, the sun shone and the plots were full of people sowing, planting and preparing their allotments for summer. I had a chat with a very friendly chap about his plot, and went home to make The Call.

The Call can be quite daunting. You're an outsider. Generally, you're ringing someone on the committee, such as the chairman. They're the allotment Big Cheese. Ron, the Burnham head honcho at the time, was no exception. He was brief, to the point and said he'd be in touch when something came up.

I was very lucky. The Burnham waiting list was short, and one nice plot holder heard that I wanted a plot. He had two, but was struggling to run them both. After waiting about a month, I got a call from Ron. I was to meet him the coming Saturday at 9.30 a.m.

Plot 105

Saturday came, and I made my way to the allotment shop. At the back of the shop stood a tall, white-haired man. He had his back to me, fiddling with some bamboo canes.

I cleared my throat. 'Er, Ron?'

Ron continued to fiddle with his canes. 'Yep.'

'I'm here to look at a plot. Jonathan, from Crouch Road?'

'Yep.'

Still Ron fiddled with the canes.

I waited for a minute or so before Ron finally turned round and checked me out. I got the feeling he was as dubious as my wife.

We took the short walk to Plot 105, passing Ron's exemplary allotment on the way. Ron and his wife, I was to learn, were allotment stalwarts of forty-odd years. They were now in charge of day-to-day running of the plots, the annual show and introducing upstarts like me to their new allotment.

To my untrained eyes, Plot 105 looked all right. It needed tidying up, for sure. There were big piles of soil and a mountain of weeds, but there was potential. Ron talked me through the rules in his gruff, to-the-point manner, before telling me to have a think about it and let him know.

I lent up against the rickety old shed. There it was. Plot 105. Ready and waiting, if I still wanted it …

Now, this begs the question: did I still want it? Of course, the answer was yes. However, things were a lot easier then. I was twenty-six, with no children or anything else that might take up my time.

I'm thirty-five now, married with two wonderful but rather wilful children. If Hugh Fearnley-Whittingstall came bounding along now, with his floppy hair and earthy recipes, would I still take on an allotment?

I've had eight amazing years on two different plots, running my own and then helping my mum with hers. Growing my own veg has been life changing. I'd absolutely, completely and wholeheartedly still take on an allotment, but I'd ponder these eight things first ...

1. Decide why you want to run an allotment

This is possibly the most important thing to think about, as you'll need a certain amount of drive. Allotments are fantastic, but they do need to become part of your life rather than something you live around; they require a commitment.

So, are you taking on your allotment to reduce your food miles or gain more control over what you eat? Are you trying to save money, or is it something to do to relax? Maybe it's the chance to grow something you might not find in the shops, or perhaps you just want to eat the tastiest, freshest fruit and veg possible?

You will need to remember this focus when you're struggling for the motivation to get down there.

2. Ease yourself in

Take your time and assess what's in front of you – it's okay to have empty beds! If you're worried about time and commitment, just grow a few things in your first year and go from there. Be realistic and you won't find yourself chasing your tail all the time. Half a dozen great harvests are much better for spirits, taste buds and wallets than a load of plants that have struggled because you've not had the time to look after them all.

3. Work out how much time you can spare

Are you generally busy Saturday mornings? When can you make the time to get down to your plot?

If you're short on time, can you work the plot with a friend? When I first took mine on, I had my mum's help, and a friend of mine works her plot with both her mum and her aunt. Another friend has a whole plot, but has given half over to a work colleague. Be realistic about how much time you'll really want to spend on the allotment.

4. What do you want to grow?

Don't worry about the things you don't eat many of. There's no pressure to grow loads of cauliflowers or sprouts just because you suddenly have the space. You should treat yourself to the fruit and veg you really love. A neighbour at my plots grows only soft fruit in summer, and then puts the patch to bed for the winter.

Remember, if you're really excited about the crops you're growing, you'll find the time to do the work you need to.

5. Get online

TV programmes are great for fuelling the passion, but they are entertainment. Blogs are realistic, and show crops dying, untidy plots and what happens when you go on holiday.

It's also worth watching some vlogs on YouTube. Again, these show real plot holders, working allotments alongside all the other stuff we have going on in our lives. And Twitter's great for getting in touch with other gardeners to exchange tips.

6. How accessible is your plot?

The key to a well-run allotment is little and often. Can you get there quickly and easily? Falling behind means long days catching up, and this can turn the plot into a chore and get you down.

7. Don't take things too seriously – it's meant to be fun!

If you're not enjoying yourself, give up and look at growing another way. There is nothing wrong with doing this!

Growing veg is a truly marvellous hobby, but to get the most from it you've got to enjoy what you're doing. A small, manageable and successful patch is much more satisfying than a scruffy allotment plot that you haven't time to look after.

Can you get creative with your space at home instead? Maybe in your front garden (like Naomi from outofmyshed.co.uk), on a balcony (check out Mark from www.verticalveg.co.uk) or growing up a wall in the backyard (see Alexandra's examples on www.rhs.org.uk/advice/grow-your-own/containers/veg-on-walls).

8. Could you grow just as effectively in your garden?

This is a biggie, for a couple of reasons. Firstly, after making The Call, you might actually find yourself on a waiting list that, quite literally, could run into years. Allotments are highly sought after in urban areas particularly, and prices are sneaking up. If you want to grow vegetables this side of the next century, you might have no choice but to look elsewhere.

If this is the case and you're lucky enough to have a garden, could you make use of the space you have there? Is there a corner that you could turn over to designated veg beds? You might not have as much space to use for veggies, but it is surprising how much can be crammed into a small area.

Secondly, does growing in your garden suit your lifestyle better? A kitchen garden is undoubtedly more convenient and time-friendly than an allotment. Being able to pop out the back door and be straight in among your plants is very handy, and makes even ten minutes' work worthwhile.

I started growing in my garden when my first child was born. My beds then were small, but that made managing my time much easier and I could split my sessions into little and often. My eldest, Lewis, now four, comes and helps me until he is bored and then just goes back into the house. If I took him to the allotment, I'd be facing a tantrum when I refused to take him home to watch *Paw Patrol* after half an hour!

Don't just limit yourself to the back garden, though. I've seen some really lovely vegetable gardens out the front of houses, particularly in cities where space is at a premium. And don't rule out making use of patios and balconies, either. Growing food in these spaces is a developing trend in urban areas, as they're normally small but sunny spaces perfect for container plants, such as tomatoes, salads, herbs and even dwarf pea and bean varieties.

Container plants need lots of water as they dry out quicker than those in the ground, and although the soil can be expensive, containers are easily found for free. I use old recycling boxes that my local council are throwing away and are the perfect size for most veg, if a little ugly.

Wine boxes are perfect for salad leaves, and old drawers make quirky but practical growing containers. Even cardboard boxes will support plants sufficiently for a season if lined inside with plastic layering.

Although these are the most common places for growing your own food, there are other options available, too. If you don't have anywhere suitable, you might be able to rent or borrow a slice of land from someone else, maybe a neighbour or even at work. A group of my colleagues set up a gardening club in the courtyard outside our office and grew flowers as well as veg in the beds.

Ten Reasons to Take on an Allotment

Now for some parity. The last thing I want to do is put you off an allotment before we've even passed Chapter One!

There is loads of information around about the benefits of growing your own fruit and veg. People far more eloquent than I will ever be have done an excellent job of explaining how the taste of homegrown food far outstrips that of shop-bought alternatives, and, of course, there are the other obvious positives, such as reduction of food miles and the chance to harvest truly delicious food at its very freshest.

These things are obvious, so I won't go over old ground. Instead, I'll give you ten other less obvious reasons for renting an allotment.

1. Extra space

If you want to grow lots and lots of fruit and veg, then an allotment will give most of us much more space than our gardens will. This is particularly useful if you're growing for a family, but also if you want to grow extra for freezing or storing. It also allows you room to be indulgent and grow loads of your favourites, like strawberry plants or fruit bushes.

2. Community

Growing in your garden can be lonely, especially if you're a sociable type. There are always plenty of people at the allotments to chat to, as well as summer shows and events. If you're lucky, you'll find yourself on a really friendly plot, where afternoon cups of tea and cake are the norm.

3. Cheap

Allotments are a bargain. At an average of £30 per year, they're probably cheaper to run than your garden. My rent was £18 a year, and I can't think of a better way to have spent that money.

4. Tips from others

Allotment holders are friendly folk, and from my experience they're always willing to pass on tips and advice to newcomers. Each allotment site will have many long-standing members, who have worked their plots for a number of years. You could fit what they don't know about growing in your soil on the back of a seed packet.

5. The allotment shop

As well as being a great hub for meeting fellow plot holders, the allotment shop will often be much cheaper than local garden centres. Many allotment societies take up the discounted seed club offers from seed merchants, meaning that seeds are sometimes as much as 50 per cent cheaper.

6. Differentiating from the garden

Having an allotment can be great for separating your spaces. Some people like to keep their gardens as a family space, for example, where the kids can run around and there's no danger of prized veg plants being flattened by a stray football.

(If only I understood when I was a kid what I understand now, I'd have behaved myself in my mum's garden a lot more …)

7. An escape from the house

At times, it's just nice to have somewhere to escape to. An allotment is a haven, somewhere away from the normal day-to-day stuff, where you can potter and ignore everything else going on in your life.

8. Seed and plant swaps

At my allotment site, there are often surplus plants left outside the front gate, free for anyone to make use of. I've also swapped lots of seeds and plants with fellow plot holders. My favourites were my globe artichokes, celeriac and the oodles of spare seed potatoes that people are always trying to find homes for.

9. The buzz of being part of something

Arriving at the allotment on a busy Saturday in spring is an exhilarating feeling. I never thought I'd be excited about the sound of lawnmowers, but together with the bustle of people getting ready for summer, it really lifts the spirits.

Some of my favourite days on the plot were when the allotments were busy like that, and often I'd just down tools and take a walk around. It was those days that reminded me how a flourishing allotment site is a really special place to be.

10. Saving money

An important factor for deciding to grow your own fruit and veg might be to reduce your weekly shopping bill and save yourself some money. The Office of National Statistics estimated that in 2016 the average family spent approximately £56.80 a week on food and drink, and with that amounting to more than £3,000 a year, it is easy to see why this might be a motive for renting an allotment or starting a kitchen garden.

Back in 2008, the National Allotment Society set out to quantify how much money could be saved by growing your own fruit and veg on an allotment plot. They gathered information on harvest weights from twenty volunteers across the United Kingdom, and plugged the results into spreadsheets.

After number-crunching the figures for over a year, the society concluded their experiments with an estimate that a handsome sum of £1,564 of fruit and veg could easily be grown on an average allotment plot over the course of a year. They also estimated that an average plot costs £202 to run per annum, which gives a tidy profit of over £1,300.

When I looked into this, I would come across people asking the same questions. 'How much can I save?' was naturally the first one, but it would regularly be followed with a 'Yeah, but ...' People wanted to believe that an allotment would save them cash, but they'd often be dubious, asking, 'Will this *really* save me anything?'

Eager to work this out myself, I started logging my harvests and trying to compare my produce to the prices I'd pay in the local supermarkets. I've been doing this since 2011, when I weighed every single one of my harvests for a year (my girlfriend thought I was nuts, but luckily she still married me).

My own findings suggested that during 2011 I'd grown around £532 of crops (when compared to the prices charged in Britain's biggest supermarket chain), and once I'd taken off my outgoings, such as compost, seeds and rent, I estimated my overall savings to be in the region of £473 for the year. It is worth noting that these savings were based on food grown purely for my wife and me. Once my two boys turn into vegetable-munching machines (a parent has to hope, right?) I reckon my savings will be even higher.

Of course, one thing you'll have to factor in is labour. A money-saving sceptic will always argue that once this is taken into account then any saving is wiped out completely. There is no doubt that allotments take graft, but growing fruit and veg is such a wonderful hobby that I don't agree that labour is something that needs to be calculated into savings. You will no doubt experience other great benefits from an allotment or vegetable plot other than purely saving money, but that doesn't mean you can't tailor how you grow towards reaping maximum cash-saving rewards.

Graft and time is kind of the deal. Everything that saves you money requires labour, whether it is fixing your own car, painting your own house or cycling to work. Growing veg is no different. If you're happy to put some time into the right things, I firmly believe that you'll see those food bills reduce dramatically, too.

Recording Your Savings

And so, the geeky bit!

The only true way to know if you've made any savings is to record them against the cost of equivalent produce in the shops. I use a spreadsheet created with the Excel computer program, with columns for the date harvested, the type of fruit or veg, the weight of the harvest and the supermarket price per kilo. There is a little formula that then works out the saving, based on the weight and the supermarket price, which automatically populates the last column. (I told you it was geeky!)

I'm no spreadsheet whizz, but if you'd like to try using mine, the latest version is available to download from my website, www.realmensow.co.uk. The spreadsheet also has sections for outgoings, which link into the other fields and are deducted from the harvest totals to give a final savings figure.

I've also found that recording savings is useful for planning the next year. It is really handy to be able to see which varieties crop well, and for how long harvests last from each sowing. This definitely focuses the mind on which crops to grow to provide the best yield, and is also an eye-opener to just how much fruit and veg costs in the shops – who'd have thought that a bog-standard leek is about £3 a kilo in the supermarkets!

I'm now on the fourth version of my spreadsheet, which also doubles as a virtual notebook. I'm not as anal as I once was, but my previous years' spreadsheets are an invaluable source of information on years gone by.

Things You'll Need

I still remember the first afternoon I spent on my allotment. I remember feeling so invigorated by the concept of having my own little space in the world. My mind was awash with ideas of what could go where, and this certainly wasn't limited to the type of crops I was going to grow. There I was, standing before an area roughly the size of two tennis courts, ready to make it my own. Lost in a dream world, I pictured a lovely old shed and nice patio area where I could sup a beer, and all the other things that help create the perfect allotment.

Fortunately, my lovely and very realistic wife was there to bring her daydreaming husband down to earth. 'You're miles from the nearest tap,' she said, pointing several plots down. 'You'll need to think about that.'

Ailsa was, of course, right. There are a number of practical things that need considering before you get started. What tools you will need, and where you will store them, for example. And how are you going to dispose of the mountains of weeds that take over the beds come summer?

Basic Tools and Equipment

Buying tools can be an expensive initial outlay, so I'd definitely recommend resisting the urge to rush to the garden centre and buy a bootful of sparkling, new gear straight away. An early wishlist of tools can easily end up as long as a prize parsnip, so take your time before deciding to splash out. Instead, spend your hard-earned cash on the three or four tools that you really need.

Spade

A spade will be your main tool for digging on the plot. A good spade can cost around £20, which I would have said was expensive until the day I snapped two cheap ones trying to shift a globe artichoke plant (much to the amusement of the onlooking and extremely more experienced neighbouring plot holders). After that rather embarrassing morning, I'd definitely say that buying the best you can is beneficial in the long run. Look out for the stainless steel models, which will be strong but light to use.

Fork

A fork is used for breaking up the soil after digging, and can also be useful for harvesting crops that grow under the soil, such as potatoes. Forks are also handy for lifting plants without damaging the roots too much. Again, a decent fork will set you back £20 – look for the stainless steel models.

Hoe

Before you know it, a good hoe will quickly become your allotment best friend. Light and versatile, a hoe is used for a number of different sowing prep purposes, including moving and preparing soil and making narrow trenches.

Primarily, however, a hoe makes light work of scooping weeds up, and you'll be grateful for not having to spend ages bent over pulling weeds out one by one. Regular use will gradually reduce the weeds in your beds, and it's best used in dry weather so that hoed weeds can't make use of the moisture in the soil to re-root.

Rake

A valuable tool for levelling your soil once you've dug it over and broken it down into a nice tilth. Use the head to drag soil around your beds so that it is equally distributed, as you go breaking down clumps that you've missed with the spade. If there's anything as satisfying as harvesting great produce in this game, it's standing back and admiring your freshly raked soil.

Trowel

Another trusty allotment friend, a trowel tackles those jobs too delicate for a spade, such as planting out seedlings, dislodging bigger weeds near to veg plants and harvesting well-established root crops without the fear of sticking a spade through them. Keep a keen eye on where you leave your trowel, though; I've lost count of the amount of times I've mislaid mine, only to find it lurking between rows of plants.

Watering Can

Most allotments discourage the use of hoses, and instead there will be various tap stations near your plot. Unless you install water butts or a big, old bath to catch rainwater, you'll need watering cans to ferry water back from the taps. Plastic watering cans are cheap, so buy two and then you can carry them both back, maximizing time and increasing biceps equally on each arm.

Make sure your watering can comes with a rose, so that you don't damage seedlings or disturb soil and newly sown seeds when watering.

Looking After Your Tools

Remember to look after your tools. Give them a decent scrub down with a wet rag from time to time and leave to dry in a warm place, like a utility room. If you've got nowhere to store them on the plot, lay them underneath a piece of tarpaulin to provide shelter from the rain. Keeping the tools dry and regularly cleaning them will prevent rust and prolong their life.

Finding Cheap Tools

If gardening on a budget, there are a few ways in which you can source cheap tools. Should your new plot have a shed, be sure to check what's been left inside before venturing to the garden centre. I inherited an old spade on my first plot, which while not being in the best nick, tided me over until I could afford something better.

Otherwise, second-hand tools can be found at jumble sales, and on websites like eBay, Gumtree, Preloved and Freecycle. It is definitely worth asking on Facebook, too

– I've found this to be invaluable when looking for plot extras and you might be surprised how many people have old tools and gardening gear clogging up their sheds that they'd be happy to get rid of.

Keep your eye out when visiting your local tip as well. One man's rubbish is another man's treasure ...

Sheds and Other Useful Bits and Bobs

As time passes, there will be plenty of other tools and paraphernalia that you'll acquire to help you on the allotment or veg patch, both big and small. You will need somewhere to keep it all, so if you're not lucky enough to inherit one on your new plot, you might decide a shed is a worthy way to invest all that cash you've saved by growing your own veg!

Sheds are ingrained in allotment culture, and plots up and down the country are full of wonderful examples of how super sheds can be. They are often reflective of their owners, and range from the neat and functional to the truly wacky. My favourite shed at my local plot is a replica of Doctor Who's blue tardis and, and on a wet and miserable winter's day, I can't help but be envious of a beautifully kept shed nearby, complete with gas stove, kettle and, no doubt, biscuits.

I adored my first shed, a rickety, old, blue thing that was wobblier than a jelly on a spacehopper and eventually gave way to high winds. It was only tiny, but seemed full of history and nostalgia, including vintage seed tins and heavy and impractical (but glorious) wooden tools. I replaced it with a modern 6 × 4 (the common way of describing a shed measuring 6 ft by 4 ft or 1.8 m by 1.2 m), which I loved equally for its tidy racking and sense of organization. Tidy shed, tidy mind and all that.

If you do invest in a shed, make sure that you give the timber a coat of preservative once a year, and replace any peeling roof felt so that rain doesn't get in. A shed is likely to be one of the most significant spends in your allotment life, so it's worth showing it a little love from time to time.

A wheelbarrow is another worthwhile purchase, especially if you can't get manure delivered right next to your plot or you can't park nearby and will need a way of transporting bags of weeds or rubbish to the car.

I'd thoroughly recommend two or three compost bins, too. Kitchen compost is a wonderful, rich organic matter that improves soil and boosts crops no end. Purpose-made dalek-style bins are compact in size and make great compost, but you can also easily make a freebie compost heap from old pallets. A bucket for gathering up weeds and old bags for taking them away in are always useful, as well as carrier bags for getting impromptu harvests home. (The amount of times I've forgotten to take some to the allotment and have had to stumble home somehow juggling numerous different vegetables …)

A ball of string covers a multitude of functions, from fastening plants to supporting stakes or tying between sticks to help sow a straight line of seeds. Gardening gloves protect hands from irritable weeds and spiky bits, and secateurs are vital for taking cuttings and clean harvesting of vine-growing crops like squashes and cucumbers.

Many GYOers (that is, those who grow your own fruit and veg) now choose to start seeds off in pots and plant out later rather than sow directly as this can help improve germination rates, as well as allowing you to start earlier in cold weather if you've got a greenhouse. Pots are cheap to buy, but second-hand pots are often found for free at many garden centres. If you do choose to grow in pots, the best growing medium is bags of multipurpose compost, available at garden centres and nurseries. Peat-free is marginally more expensive but has improved greatly over the years and is much better for the environment.

And don't forget somewhere to sit and mull over allotment life or take a rest in the middle of a hard session of digging. A folding picnic chair is perfect and easily storable in a small shed, or you might want to get a bit more creative. I use a nice big lump of driftwood perched on two large logs for my plot relaxation and vantage point, but my favourite is an old pub bench on an allotment plot I visited in Dorset, complete with paving slabs, parasol and pot plants.

I can never keep up with all the other little things that I've bought for the plot. My shed is full of stuff that I've accumulated, such as bamboo canes for supporting tall, twining plants and rolls of mesh netting to keep the cabbage whites off my brassicas, but the above list will give you the basics and get you growing.

CHAPTER 2

How Not to Spend Money on the Allotment

Saving money by growing fruit and veg on an allotment is not just about the value of the food you produce. If your aim is to chip away at the monthly food bill, that has to be balanced against what you spend fulfilling your objective. Although I guarantee you'll have lots of good times and delicious, fresh produce, the aim of financial frugality is blown out of the water if the money saved in food is wiped out by spending £600 on allotment equipment.

There are some things that you won't be able to do without, like those we covered in the previous chapter. Unless you like burrowing with your hands, tools such as spades and trowels, for example, are indispensable. However, with some imagination, opportunism and good old-fashioned bartering, you can reduce considerably what you spend on growing veg.

Apart from the vegetables themselves, one of the most invigorating elements of running an allotment is this challenge of keeping costs down. A walk around any local allotments will reveal umpteen inspiring and innovative ways people have repurposed items to utilize in their growing adventure. Just on my local plots I have seen wonderful examples, from homemade sheds to potatoes growing in old tyres, beautiful driftwood benches and plants climbing up an unwanted kids' football goal. I've also come across some brilliant veg beds made from wardrobes, wooden dinghies and bathtubs, as well as my absolute favourite: a raised bed made from a – yep, you guessed it – a bed!

The beauty of allotment upcycling is that you don't need to be especially creative, able to turn the most tired looking piece of junk into a work of art. Equally, you don't have to be particularly handy. For more ambitious projects it helps to know your way around a saw and a spirit level, but most of the time it's about a bit of graft and a willingness to get the boot of your car grubby transporting dirty, old things to your plot. And if you're not creative, then just do what I do and copy stuff you see on the internet!

Essentially, items you repurpose on an allotment don't have to win you any art competitions. They just have to *work*. If there's one place in the world where an old, discarded eighties' bathtub doesn't look out of the ordinary, it's an allotment. When something is free and solves a problem you'd otherwise have had to spend money on, then anything goes.

And while the internet is full of inspirational, big DIY projects such as greenhouses made from plastic bottles and two-storey shed mansions built out of pallets, the little things become equally important to the allotment holder on a budget. Annual purchases of seeds, labels, pots, potting compost, netting and all the other everyday items add up, but with some thought these are all things that can be replicated for free or bought cheaply. From my experience, if you're prepared to do slightly bonkers things like routinely gathering up all the toilet roll inners from the toilets at work, you needn't spend a penny on growing food. As it were.

Once upon a winter's night, I was indulging in some late-night, allotment-based web browsing. I had just come out of the other side of my veg-weighing year, and like most blokes, was looking for a new project. I stumbled across a post on an allotment forum where a gentleman said that he loved gardening, but he didn't like it to cost him too much money. He took great pride and enjoyment from the challenge of keeping things frugal, and particularly the resourcefulness and creativity that this approach relied on. In fact, the gentleman even went as far as to say that he didn't like to spend more than £5 a month on his garden. I read this with great interest – a fiver a month, now there was a challenge ...

I spent some time trying this. Some months I crept outside my limit, but generally I was close. I used all manner of freebie alternatives to items I'd normally buy, both big and small, and started keeping a record of all the tips for keeping costs down that I discovered or used myself. I had a pad that became my little black book of money-saving objects, and I'd jot down ideas and advice for keeping my spend small.

One of the great things about allotments is that there is a functional reason for their existence so the pressure to spend money on beautiful things isn't as pressing as it might be in, say, a garden, where you might want it to be a bit more decorative. This provides the resourceful allotmenteer with licence to use all manner of free or inexpensive bits and bobs to help with the everyday running of a plot while keeping costs to a minimum. Allotment holders are indeed a resourceful bunch, and I've seen many wonderful examples of reduce, reuse and recycle. This chapter details some of my favourite tips and tricks for turning easily found, common items into useful veg-growing tools, and giving them a whole new lease of life while you're at it.

Using Household Rubbish

The challenge for a frugal allotment holder is to break down a conundrum, and work out how to solve it without spending very much. A good way of doing this is to find out what is available to buy, and then try to find a readily available free or cheap alternative that will do the same job. This can often take some fiddling and fixing to achieve, but some things are straight swaps. For example, horticultural fleece can set you back a pound a metre, but bubble wrap will do the job just as well, so next time you receive a parcel, remember to store the wrapping away to use in the winter.

In fact, our homes, sweet homes are one of the most fertile places for finding free things for the allotment. The cardboard insides of toilet rolls can be used for growing seeds in modules by cutting the tubes in half or thirds, filling with multipurpose compost and planting the whole thing out once the seed germinates. The cardboard will simply rot down into the soil leaving the seedling to grow on. Yoghurt pots can also be used instead of the conventional red or black pots to grow seedlings – just make sure you stab some holes in the bottom for drainage.

Cleaning up three or four margarine tubs and cutting the plastic into plant labels should see you through a season's sowing, and although there won't be much room for fancy, free-flowing italics, it will easily save a fiver. Cut

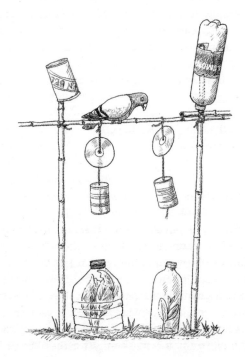

the labels with a pointed edge at the bottom to help poke them into the soil.

Big squash bottles are great for turning into cloches for frost protection and early sowings. Simply cut one in half and slot it over the young plant. They might not be as stylish and attractive as a purpose-made cloche, but they're not £30 either. Pricking holes in the lid of a squash bottle also creates a very passable watering can with a fine rose head for use on delicate seedlings.

These very same bottles can also be used as watering traps by cutting in half and burying the top half upside down next to the base of a plant. Push the bottle down so the cut edge is level with the soil, and then fill up with water. The water will slowly be released into the soil over a period of time, rather than running off so the soil dries out before the water can take effect. This method also ensures that the water gets in and around the plant, right where you want it.

Plastic milk bottles and drink cans make very useful safety covers for the tops of pointy sticks and canes, and double up as effective bird-scarers when they rattle in the wind. Old CDs tied to lines of string also provide an effective deterrent to the birds.

Skips and Tips

For the eagle-eyed, neighbourhood skips can be a veritable goldmine of allotment goodies. More often than not, a skip will be full of old wood, which can easily be turned into something useful for the plot. Scaffold boards are perfect for raised beds, while discarded wooden boxes and drawers are great for container-growing and carry a certain rustic charm. They're perfect for salad and other leafy veg and being mobile, you can start them off early indoors before

moving them outside when things warm up. My favourite boxes are old wine boxes, but even a stray piece of wood can be cut up and banged into a presentable planter.

If you're short on space but want to grow some potatoes, they grow well in old bags and sacks. Hessian sacks, plastic multipurpose compost or soil bags and builders' bags will all harbour a bumper spud crop and can be found in pretty much any skip or tip.

Look out for windows being thrown away, as these make very functional coldframes if laid on top of a square of bricks, and grab any mesh-like net that you see. They are just the job for protecting plants from pests such as cabbage white butterflies. The best I've used is old net curtains, but scaffold netting runs it close.

You'll regularly find soil being tipped into skips, too, and while this might not be grade A quality, it will be handy for bulking up raised beds and containers. I filled my garden's raised beds from soil that was dug up by a neighbour when building a driveway, and mixed it with compost, manure and other improvers to create a really nice growing medium.

Pallets have a multitude of uses, but are most commonly used to make a compost heap. Nail three together on their sides to form an open box shape, cram your old plants, grass cuttings and paper inside and cover with an old carpet or tarpaulin. Another option for a free compost bin is to use an old dustbin, with a small door cut out at the bottom to release the decomposed material.

All you need is some imagination, and a skip can present lots of money-saving opportunities, but of course, remember the skip-diving rules: skips on driveways are strictly out of bounds, and ask before you make off with anything!

Another place to keep your eyes peeled is the local tip. Large pots, containers and even unwanted plants regularly turn up at the tip. Old carpet or tarpaulin can be used to cover up soil to suppress weeds in the winter, as can large sheets of cardboard. Cardboard is really handy for laying over any part of a plot that is a work in progress, as it composts down into the soil as well as preventing weeds from growing up. Television boxes are the perfect size, and my local tip is full of them.

Seeds

One of the biggest annual expenses when running an allotment is seeds, and if you're growing to save money, keeping the cost of your seed down is going to be very important. The good news is that getting hold of free or cheap packets of seeds is actually very easy if you're prepared to put a bit of legwork in.

Magazine freebies are an excellent place to start, and seem to get better and better with each passing year. Around sowing time there will often be six packets included for free with an issue of a gardening magazine, and not only

does this mean each packet will cost you less than a pound, you'll get all the tips and advice from the magazine, too.

Some seed companies offer discounted rates to allotment and gardening societies, meaning seed prices in the allotment shops and committee sheds are cheaper than the nurseries and online retailers. I'm lucky enough to have an allotment shop on site, and seeds are normally between 40 and 50 per cent cheaper than the shops. If you don't have an allotment shop, many seed companies offer these discounted rates to seed-buying groups as well as allotment societies. Find enough people prepared to join your group, and you'll be able to take advantage of these special prices, too.

The local Pound Shop is also worth a nose for the budget-conscious grower. Every town has one, and although the ranges are generally limited, seeds normally start from around 75p a packet.

Seed-swapping is very popular, especially given the amount of seeds that come in a packet. A typical carrot packet will hold a thousand seeds, far beyond what even the most carrot-keen allotment holder will be able to sow in a summer. Instead, keep some back for a seed-swapping day. A quick search on the internet will bring up plenty of places to take unused seeds and exchange them for ones you do need, but if you can't find one nearby, why not set up your own? Local newspapers and newsletters enjoy these types of stories, and a quick email to the editor together with a few posters will get the coverage required to ensure enough people come along. I love seed-swapping events, as they're like a grown-up version of football stickers (got … got … need … got).

Nowadays, of course, all this can be done virtually. Most internet gardening forums have seed-swapping sections which I have used to not only grab what's on offer, but also post some wanted threads. Social media networks are great communities to become part of, where lots of wonderful and friendly gardeners congregate to discuss vegetables and seed-swapping buddies can be found in no time at all. Twitter is especially good – explore the #allotment hashtag for links to lots of other growers.

As you become a more confident and experienced gardener, you may want to save seeds from your own crops. This is an easy way of saving money each year, especially if you concentrate on the more expensive seeds such as peas, beans and squashes. As luck would have it, these are also the easiest seeds to save. To save peas and beans, leave some pods on the plants after harvesting, and wait for them to dry out. You will know when this has happened, as the pods will become crispy and brown. Pick out the seeds and keep them in a sealed envelope. It is vital that the seeds are stored somewhere airtight as they will deteriorate fast if exposed to moisture, so pop the envelopes into a sealed container over the winter. Remember to label the variety and year for reference.

Squashes are equally easy to save. Simply dig out the seeds when preparing the squash and set aside for them to dry. Store in an envelope just like beans and peas.

Another advantage of saving your own seed is that you will essentially be developing your own strain, which over time will become more accustomed to your environment than seeds you buy in the shops.

Friends and Facebook

One of the most successful ways of getting useful things for your allotment adventure is one of the simplest and best: making friends and chewing the cud. It's amazing how often a conversation about growing vegetables can lead to favours being exchanged and offers of freebie swapsies.

One of my favourite places to start is at work, as it never ceases to amaze me how many closet veg growers can exist quietly in an organization. Once word gets around, there is never a shortage of people to chat with. Facebook is also a brilliant resource for making use of things that others don't want. A quick post one evening can soon lead to a problem solved. I've been given unwanted compost bins, builders' bags, manure, scaffold boards and plants among many other useful paraphernalia, simply by asking nicely if anyone had any they wanted rid of. I even got an old bathtub delivered to my plot by a plumber I used to play football with. Old bathtubs make excellent butts for holding water if you've got no tap close to your allotment.

Make Your Own Multipurpose Compost

Another annual cost will be multipurpose compost for sowing seeds. Large sacks of good quality compost can be quite expensive and if you choose to start seeds off in pots, you can easily work through half a dozen of the 50-litre packs and leave a big deficit in your growing budget before you've even started.

When I was experimenting with my fiver-a-month expenditure limit, I decided to explore making my own compost for sowing. I mostly used homemade stuff and found that if you're already composting kitchen scraps and leaves, producing your own compost is actually really easy. All you need is a garden sieve (available cheaply from most garden centres), and equal parts leaf mulch, kitchen compost and soil. For the soil, I scooped up a few bags of molehill soil from the local common. Sieve everything together as and when you're preparing to sow, and hey presto, beautiful, crumbly soil for next to nothing.

The only downside is that using unsterilized, homemade soil will make weeds in your pots unavoidable, but a gentle pricking out of infant weeds once a week is small price to pay for free compost and the satisfaction of making it yourself.

Homemade Plant Food

A potent, nutrient-packed plant food can be made easily and stinkily using regular stinging nettles, comfrey, or a mixture of both. All you need is a bucket and some gloves to gather the stingers. Half fill the bucket with nettles, fill up with water and leave for a couple of weeks until the concoction becomes very pungent. Once you're satisfied with the stench, use the food at a ratio of about eight parts water to each part smelly food. Nettles are full of nitrogen, which is particularly good for leafy crops.

Another unlikely and potentially unpopular choice for free plant food is urine. Urine is an excellent compost activator, and is particularly good at breaking down the

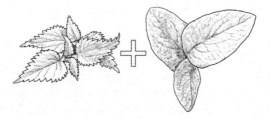

browns in compost, such as twigs and cardboard. Just make sure you relieve yourself privately into a transporting vessel, or you might find your allotment membership under threat …

Buy and Sell Groups and the Allotment

Freecycle, eBay and local Facebook Buy and Sell groups are all a good source of second-hand tools, compost bins and timber. Manure will also pop up from time to time, as will bigger but more complicated things like greenhouses. Dismantling a greenhouse can be a tricky affair, but the rewards are great. Watch out for brittle glass, and if you do need any new panes, a local glass company will cut some to size for you at a reasonable price. Given that even a budget greenhouse can cost £300, the chance to relocate one for free isn't to be sniffed at.

The allotments themselves can be productive places for finds, and most people are more than happy to share within the growing community. At my local allotments, unwanted items are left outside the hut with 'free to a good home' signs. I have been lucky enough to pick up a couple of dalek compost bins and a big bag of rhubarb crowns in the past, but remember that it works both ways – be sure to return the favour whenever you can.

CHAPTER 3

Growing Guides

Once upon a time, I used to plan my allotment or veg plot around factors such as how many beds I could fit in or how much space I had to play with. I'd dig over every bed before I even had an idea of what to sow in there. It seemed the logical thing to do. I had a load of space on my allotment, and I was going to fill the whole lot! The thing was, I often didn't end up using all the beds I had prepared. There was only so much I could grow, or needed to grow. One day, slumped over my spade in the rain, I realized that I was doing it the wrong way round.

I had been busy making a runner bean trench. Runner bean plants need very rich soil, so one growing tactic is to dig a trench at the beginning of winter and fill it with kitchen scraps, grass cuttings and pulled-up, old veg plants that would all compost down. Towards the end of winter, you fill in the trench with soil, ready to plant the runner beans on top.

This was the first time I'd prepared an area for a specific crop, and once I'd realized this, I straightaway changed the way I planned my plot. So, before doing anything else, I wrote a list of the crops I wanted to grow, and then designed the beds around them, rather than haphazardly filling the space with plants. It was a much more focused, logical and time-efficient way of doing things, helping me work out the amount of space I actually required – and very handy when I began growing crops in my garden.

Ever since, I've waited for a suitably cold and miserable winter's night to light the fire, make a cup of tea and compose a list of veg I'd like to grow the following year. Once I've got this licked, I start planning the plot: where I'll sow, whether there are any particular soil demands, how many rows I need and other important factors, such as which of my crops might cope best in the shady parts.

Growers will need to know the intricacies of each plant before they start their planning. The good news is that most simply enjoy good soil, water, sun and some protection from a few choice pests. I've put together this growing guide that includes what I believe are the most reliable and rewarding plants for beginners to grow. There isn't anything particularly exotic or fancy in there, just common, solid fruit, veg and herbs that will get you up and running and enjoying solid and delicious harvests in your first year and beyond.

Beetroot

One thing I've quickly come to appreciate on the allotment is the unsung hero veg. Growing attention-seeking plants is all well and good, but sooner rather than later you'll grow to love those veg with great productivity versus faff ratios. With big, easy-to-handle seeds that make for simple sowing and few demands, beetroot is one such crop. Once in the ground, you could almost leave them be.

They require a little watering at seedling stage, but then they just seem to grow, whatever the conditions. Year in, year out, the trusty beet has been ever-present in my veg beds, quietly producing excellent yields over and over again while I fret about the sulking tomatoes or the slugs eating fifty times their body weight in other seedlings.

If you want to spend a little time in the company of

your baby beetroots, you can thin out the seedlings and transplant them into gaps or elsewhere on the plot. Water in, and beetroot seedlings will happily take and grow on to boost your bumper beet harvest and increase the productivity versus faff ratio even more. Being expensive to buy in the shops, this tactic also brings further cash savings.

Excess beetroots can be preserved for winter by boiling and pickling in airtight jars and then using in salads. Beets are more versatile in the kitchen than you might think, too: there are recipes knocking about for hummus, Nordic-inspired beetroot burgers and risotto, although I'd draw the line at brownies, particularly if you prefer your chocolatey treats sweet rather than slightly soily!

Seeds are best sown directly 2 cm (0.8 in) deep in well-prepared soil. Try sowing under cloches (plastic bottles cut in half for freebie option) in late winter for the chance of an early harvest, otherwise repeated sowings every two to four weeks from March until July will provide a regular harvest throughout summer and autumn. Thin seedlings to 10 cm (4 in) apart.

When to Sow
March to July

Spacing
Allow 30 cm (1 ft) between each row

Time to Harvest
12–16 weeks

Recommended Varieties
Boltardy, Detroit Crimson. Cylindra is a cylindrical-shaped variety, which is lovely for slicing

Advantages
Expensive to buy in the shops, reliable, easy to grow, gluts can be preserved

Disadvantages
Not quite as versatile in the kitchen as some other veg

Top Tip
Replant thinnings for extra crops as roots will easily take
if kept watered

Broad Beans

An early-season favourite of allotment holders, broad beans
are a good choice for money-saving veg while waiting for
the bounty of summer. Some varieties are hardy, so can be
sown in autumn for a very early crop from May onwards,
which can be harvested until you need the space for other
later plants.

Sowing in autumn also produces tougher plants, which
are less susceptible to blackfly, a common broadie nemesis.
Aquadulce Claudia is the best variety for September to
February sowing. Sow seeds at a depth of 5 cm (2 in), 20
cm (8 in) apart, and cover with a plastic bottle cut in half
for winter protection, or in pots in a coldframe. To prevent
seeds rotting over the winter, use an area of the plot that
drains well. For later crops, sow from March onwards in a
sunny spot at the same depth and spacing.

The plants are remarkably hardy, and will survive
a frost or two even if planted out in early spring. I once
planted out a couple of very early rows before checking
the weather forecast. It snowed the next day. The plants
looked so sorry for themselves I felt compelled to write
them a letter of apology via my blog. To my amazement
they perked up once the snow melted away and went on
to produce a more than passable crop. Some of these veg
plants never cease to amaze me.

I'd still suggest tuning into the weather forecast before
planting anything out, though …

Broad beans require support, so either poke a cane into the ground next to each plant and tie cane and plant together, or plant in blocks of two rows. Put canes in at all corners of the block, and tie string between each cane for the plants to grow up.

To deter blackfly, pinch off the growing tips when the plants are flowering and the first pods have set. Blackfly can quickly grab hold of a plant, so check daily and spray any infestation with warm, soapy water.

Harvest when the pods are about 8 cm (3 in) long and freeze any surplus.

When to Sow
September to December for overwintering, February undercover, or March to May

Spacing
60 cm (24 in) between each double row

Time to Harvest
12–16 weeks for spring-sown, 26–30 weeks for autumn-sown

Recommended Varieties
Aquadulce Claudia is the best variety for overwintering. Jubilee Hysor, The Sutton

Advantages
Good yields, early crops, freeze well

Disadvantages
Susceptible to blackfly

Cabbages (Winter)

If you prefer a proper, hearty cabbage, then winter cabbages are grown in the same way as spring greens, except sown earlier. Winter cabbages take many forms, including savoy, red and hardy white varieties.

I prefer growing winter cabbages to summer cabbages, as there are more valuable crops to dedicate space to in summer, but some winter cabbages are certainly worth growing during winter.

Sow seeds directly or in pots 1 cm (0.5 in) deep in late spring. Thin to 60 cm (24 in) apart, or plant out to a similar distance if transplanting from pots.

Winter cabbages can be a magnet for cabbage white butterflies, which lay their eggs on the plants. The resulting caterpillars will chomp through a whole row in no time at all. Netting your plants will help keep the butterflies from landing and laying.

When to Sow
February to May

Spacing
30 cm (1 ft) between rows

Time to Harvest
30–35 weeks

Recommended Varieties
January King (white), Drumhead (red), Celtic (Savoy)

Advantages
Provide a harvest during winter, can leave in the ground during winter and harvest when you need them

Disadvantages
Susceptible to cabbage white butterflies

Top Tip
If you can make friends with some scaffolders, their mesh netting makes perfect protection from cabbage whites

Carrots

The biggest obstacle facing carrots is stony soil. For productive harvests, carrots need good-quality soil, free of stones. Stony soil will split the roots as they grow down or stunt the root completely. If you're a keen carrot-cultivator there's nothing more disappointing than spying a fat-looking carrot top poking through the soil, only to find nothing more than a nubbin waiting underground.

So what's the solution for keeping your carrots on the straight and hopefully not so narrow? Well, after several seasons of carrots that resembled the bottom half of a three-legged man I actually ditched the idea of growing on the allotment and tried growing carrots in containers filled with multipurpose compost. The theory was that I could control the condition of the soil, and filter out anything that might upset the carrots. This is a popular method among container-growers, and with regular watering it worked a treat. No more were my carrots stoned.

Florists' buckets are a good size for container carrots, and can be had for free from a friendly local flower seller or supermarket. You can keep the cost of filling the buckets down by mixing the compost with soil from your garden or allotment.

Carrots are susceptible to carrot fly, but planting in containers will cunningly help reduce attacks as the females of these pests cannot fly above 60 cm (2 ft). Strong-smelling plants such as leeks and mint are also useful deterrents if grown nearby.

Like potatoes, carrots are broadly separated into early and maincrop varieties. Earlies are quicker growing and can be sown all through summer, while the late varieties are slower to mature but have bigger roots and store better over winter.

Although carrots don't take up as much room as potatoes, they are also very cheap to buy so you might want to consider giving up the space to a more valuable crop.

A good carrot money-saving tactic is to sow a row of earlies under a piece of horticultural fleece in February, and again in late summer when space becomes available after pulling up spring plants. This will give both an early crop and a row of carrots that you can leave in the ground into winter to harvest as you need them, but will not impact on the growing space during peak summer months.

The seeds are paper-thin, so try to avoid sowing when the weather is blowing a hoolie. Direct sow 1–2 cm (less than an inch) deep, in well-prepared and as stone-free soil as you can get it. There are thousands of seeds in a carrot packet, so sow liberally to increase germination chances and thin seedlings out to 10 cm (4 in) apart later on.

When to Sow
Early spring to late autumn

Spacing
Allow 30 cm (1 ft) between each row

Time to Harvest
9+ weeks for earlies, 11 weeks for maincrops

Recommended Varieties
Early Nantes or Chantenay for earlies, Autumn King for best chance of a high-yielding maincrop. Parmex, a baby spherical variety, is good for quick-growing container or border sowings

Advantages
Can be left in the ground during winter, providing a valuable crop when there is little else available

Disadvantages
Very cheap to buy in the shops, can be unreliable if you have stony soil

Top Tip
Wait until the carrots are pencil-thick before thinning, and use the thinnings in salads

Courgettes

Summer just wouldn't be summer on the allotment without a courgette glut! Known for their huge number of fruits, a single plant can easily yield twenty courgettes a season.

The plants are very easy to grow, but beware of planting out too many – any more than two or three plants will leave a family swimming in courgettes. Plants take up lots of space, too, and will need at least a square metre or square yard each.

The unfussy courgette plant is a beginner's dream. I have very fond memories of growing courgettes during my first allotment year. I raised three plants and they all grew beautifully. Very little else went to plan in my first year, but my courgettes made me feel sky high. They gave me confidence that, yes, I could learn this growing your own stuff.

If you're just starting out on the road to allotment glory, I'd definitely recommend putting courgettes on the top of your seed-buying list. The fruits will become one of your biggest harvests, and hopefully give you the sense of pride I felt when I wandered back home with a bag full of courgettes.

In high summer, keep harvesting every day. A courgette will grow noticeably between morning and evening, and they are best eaten when 10–15 cm (4–6 in) long. The speed with which a courgette has grown while I've been away for the day has genuinely made me jump.

Sow and grow courgettes in the same way as squashes, planted out after the last frost, in a manure-filled recess. Keep well watered.

When to Sow
April to May

Spacing
Minimum of 1 m (3–4 ft) between plants

Time to Harvest
8–12 weeks

Recommended Varieties
Defender, Parador for yellow, nuttier flavoured fruits

Advantages
Heavy croppers, versatile in the kitchen

Disadvantages
Take up a lot of space

Top Tip
Keep a good distance between bushes so that air can
circulate, preventing mildew building up on the leaves

Cucumbers (Outdoor)

Although not as aesthetically pleasing as a proper
cucumber, outdoor varieties don't need as much warmth
as a normal cue. I started growing outdoor cucumbers on
my first allotment, when I didn't have a greenhouse.

Essentially, outdoor cucumbers are big gherkins, and
share the same rough skins, but the idea is not to let them
grow to the same size as the cucumbers you'd find in the
shops. Don't expect beautifully straight specimens – these
outdoor ones are definitely the ugly sisters of the cucumber
family, but the fruits taste every bit as good as their more
traditional siblings. If the spiky skin does put you off, try
a hybrid or Japanese variety, which produce fruits with
smoother skin.

Bush and vine varieties are available, but the vines
are more productive, and being trailing plants you can
grow them upwards to save space. Try planting them on
the corners of beds so you can easily trail the vines up a
structure or around your paths.

Start cues off in little pots of multipurpose compost,
and plant out once the risk of frost has passed. Make sure
you water regularly, and harvest the fruits when about
15 cm (6 in) long, or half the length of a conventional
cucumber.

In wet weather it can be worth putting straw under the
fruits to stop rotting and discolouration. A small handful
just to keep the fruit off the ground is perfect.

When to Sow
April to May

Spacing
60 cm (2 ft) between plants

Time to Harvest
12–14 weeks

Recommended Varieties
The tremendously named Burpless Tasty Green, or Kyoto for smooth-skinned fruits

Advantages
Heavy croppers, can grow vertically to save space

Disadvantages
A bit ugly …

Top Tip
At the end of the season, harvest any undersized cucumbers as gherkins, and pickle for Christmas

French Beans (Dwarf)

French beans are an allotment holder's dream: they're very easy to grow, require little attention and produce a prolific harvest. Dwarf bean varieties are best, as they take up less space – the yield from a small row is quite staggering, especially given how little effort these plants require.

If space is limited, French beans are a good alternative to runner beans as the plants tolerate poorer soil. Early sowings need to be made under cloches or indoors in pots for planting out later as the plants are susceptible to frost. Direct sow at a depth of 4–5 cm (1½–2 in), 20 cm (8 in) apart. The plants are fragile, so sow two rows 25 cm (10 in) apart in a sheltered but sunny spot and once big enough they will support each other. They're so low-maintenance, they even hold each other up!

For pot sowing, sow three seeds in a pot 15 cm (6 in) wide and plant out when the seedlings are 15–20 cm (6–8 in) high.

French beans have a long cropping period of up to two months, so sow at four-week intervals between April and July for harvests until autumn. The beans freeze well, too, so try to bonus-sow at the end of July in order to freeze a harvest for winter.

When to Sow
April undercover, May to July outside

Spacing
25 cm (10 in)

Time to Harvest
8–12 weeks

Recommended Varieties
Tendergreen, Speedy for quick cropping plants

Advantages
Easy and reliable, expensive in the shops, high yields, excellent use of space, freeze well

Disadvantages
None!

Top Tip
Keep on top of the harvest! French beans are best eaten young as they will become stringy if left to get too big. They crop vigorously, so the plants need checking every couple of days

Kale (Curly)

All hail curly kale! This terrifically hardy leafy green is a real Mr Dependable, surviving all types of weather to provide regular harvests through winter. It is easy to grow, although it does warrant netting from cabbage white butterflies during the summer. They love the sweet cabbage leaves as much as I do. And that's a lot.

Kale has become one of my Desert Island veg. Not only does it stand up to winter weather, it provides a steady crop through to spring, is incredibly healthy, boasts a long harvesting season and being a 'cut-and-come-again' plant, will keep cropping as you pick.

The plants don't mind poor soil, will tolerate shade, and happily shrug off even the lowest of temperatures – in fact the leaves sweeten after a frost so it is worth waiting until colder weather for the first harvests.

Sow seeds in pots from March to June at a depth of 1–2 cm (less than an inch), and transplant to the veg beds once the seedlings are 20 cm (8 in) high, 60 cm (2 ft) apart. Plant deeply and push soil down firmly around the base to give solid support. Consider staking on exposed sites unless cultivating dwarf varieties, which do not grow on a large stalk and therefore are better protected from windy weather.

Grow at least six plants on the plot to allow you to alternate harvests and give plants a rest in turn during the winter.

When to Sow
March to May

Spacing
60 cm (2 ft) between rows

Time to Harvest
25–30 weeks

Recommended Varieties
Reflex, Dwarf Green Curled, Redbor for a striking purple colour, Nero di Toscana for some variety

Advantages
Reliable, cut-and-come-again, hardy, easy to grow

Disadvantages
Susceptible to cabbage white butterflies during the summer

Top Tip
Mix in with Nero di Toscana, another delicious kale variety. Equally as easy to grow, but the leaves are sweeter

Leeks

There can be no greater allotment smell than the pungent aroma of a freshly harvested leek. It's a wonderfully heady fragrance that really confirms the superiority of homegrown produce over shop-bought equivalents. For extra leek indulgence, harvest early in the morning and leave the stems in your car while you go to work. Yes, I have accidentally done this and the smell can only be described as 'intoxicating'. And long-lasting.

As well as functioning as a veggie Magic Tree air freshener, leeks boast other useful and worthy qualities, too. They are pricey in the shops, easy to grow and can be left in the ground for autumn and winter harvesting as and when you need them.

To grow, fill a pot with multipurpose compost, sprinkle seeds liberally on top and then cover with another centimetre of compost. Once the baby leeks are pencil-thick, they're ready to plant out. Choose well-draining soil to avoid rotting.

Dibbing is the best method for planting out. This involves planting the leeks into a hole created by a dibber (a pointed wooden stick). Dibbers can be bought from garden centres, but I use the end of an old broom.

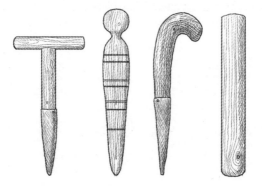

Water the soil where the leeks are to be planted, and make holes 10–15 cm (4–6 in) deep, 10 cm (4 in) apart. Turn the pot of leeks out and carefully prize them apart, before dropping a leek into each hole. Gently push the leek down the hole until you feel it touch the bottom. To get the roots right down, you might need to pull the leek up and down a few times, or use another dibbing-type instrument to poke them into place. Don't refill the hole with soil, as the leek will grow into the space.

When to Sow
March to April

Spacing
30 cm (1 ft) between rows

Time to Harvest
26–40 weeks. Thin-shanked varieties are quicker than their thick counterparts

Recommended Varieties
Autumn Mammoth for big shanks, Musselburgh for
reliability

Advantages
Good use of winter bed space, will keep in the ground
until you need them, expensive to buy, versatile in the
kitchen

Disadvantages
None!

Top Tip
Plant out some late leeks in July. They won't grow very
big over winter, but once spring comes they'll get a
growth spurt and help fill the Hungry Gap

Lettuce and Salad Leaves

What's the difference between a loose-leaf lettuce and a
hearting lettuce? Sadly there is no punchline here, simply a
couple of important-to-know definitions. Loose-leaf are cut-
and-come-again types, grown for the leaves, while hearting
are lettuces that grow a head and are picked as one.

The good news is that both are easy to grow – if you can
keep the slugs off. Most will tolerate some shade, and are
also good choices for container-growing or intercropping.
With careful seed selection, you can also enjoy salad leaves
in winter.

Sow seeds directly, 1 cm (½ in) deep, every 3–4 weeks
during spring, summer and autumn. The easiest and best
value way of doing this is to buy packets of mixed loose-
leaf seeds, sow liberally and harvest once the leaves are big
enough to make salads. The plants will be cut-and-come-
again, so keep harvesting until they go to seed.

If growing hearting varieties, thin to 10 cm (4 in) once the seedlings are established. You can transplant thinnings elsewhere.

In late summer, sow oriental leaves such as mibuna and mizuna. These hardy leaves carry a peppery kick, and will survive grotty winter conditions; the only weather that tends to finish off my crop is a sizeable dump of snow. If you can find a cloche to pop over the leaves while the white stuff drops then they will easily survive, and if you've got a greenhouse, even better.

Keep both loose-leaf and hearting lettuce well watered, especially in dry periods.

When to Sow
March to August for traditional varieties, August and September for oriental leaves

Spacing
20 cm (8 in) between rows

Time to Harvest
8–12 weeks

Recommended Varieties
Buy packets of mixed seeds for spring, summer and autumn; mibuna and mizuna for winter leaves. Little Gem and Kos for headed varieties

Advantages
Easy to grow, don't take up much space, cut-and-come-again, available all year round, good for intercropping

Disadvantages
Pretty cheap in the shops

Top Tip
Try sowing in garden borders or containers if space is an issue

Mangetout

Once upon a time, I always grew peas. You cannot beat the taste of a fresh-podded pea, straight from the plant. The trouble was, they always seemed such a fiddle, and once picked, podded and prepared, the returns underwhelmed me.

Then I discovered mangetout, a flatter variety grown to be harvested before the peas form. There are a number of advantages to this, such as less time getting the peas ready for the table and a bigger yield. Mangetout is also much more expensive to buy, whereas peas are so incredibly cheap that a huge bag of freshly frozen peas can be bought for less than a packet of seeds.

Gradually, mangetout has replaced peas in my veg beds, and successional sowings every six weeks from February provide crops into autumn. Mangetout freezes well, so any glut is put in the freezer for winter.

Mangetout are hardy enough to sow in autumn for overwintering, but February sowings benefit from some cover (cut plastic bottles in half and place over the seeds if you haven't got a greenhouse or coldframe). If sowing direct, choose a sunny spot and push the seeds in at a depth of about 4 cm (1½ in). Mangetout enjoy rich soil, so make sure it is well manured beforehand.

You can also raise mangetout in pots to plant out into open ground. Sow three seeds in a pot just 15 cm (6 in) wide to save on compost, and plant out once the seedlings are 5–10 cm (2–4 in) high, with a gap of 10 cm (4 in) between each seedling. Water the pots before planting to help keep as much soil around the roots as possible when separating the seedlings.

Support the plants with old twigs and raspberry canes or netting intertwined through bamboo canes, depending on how high your chosen variety grows.

When to Sow
February to August, September for overwintering

Spacing
Allow 75 cm (30 in) between each row

Time to Harvest
12–14 weeks

Recommended Varieties
Oregon Sugar Pod, Carouby de Maussane

Advantages
Easy and reliable, expensive in the shops, high-cropping

Disadvantages
None that I know of

Top Tip
Try growing a tall variety vertically up a wigwam of canes to maximize space. Tie string around the outside for the plants to pull themselves up on

Onions

With onions so cheap to buy in the shops, giving summer space over to them does not add up unless you eat a stack of onions. However, onions can be overwintered and a few rows in otherwise empty beds to be harvested and stored in spring are a worthy addition to your allotment, especially as the harvest will be out of the ground before summer crops are planted out.

Homegrown onions are incredibly potent, too – if you think shop-bought alternatives made you cry, wait until you cut into your first one from the veg patch ...

Onions can be grown from seed, but it is much easier and far less fiddly to buy and plant onion sets. These are little bulbs that have already enjoyed several weeks of growth, and are readily available in bags from garden centres, allotment shops and online.

Plant onion bulbs tip upwards, 5–10 cm (2–4 in) apart. Prevent birds from pinching the bulbs by pushing them into the ground so that the tip is only just on show. Don't worry about protecting the growing onions over winter, and don't fret if growth is slow either. They'll soon bulk up once warmer weather arrives.

Harvest when the tops die off and bend over, and leave to dry out before storing, ready for use as and when. Onions are easy to store on shelves or plaited together and hung up, but make sure they're in a frost-free environment.

When to Plant
Late summer for overwintering

Spacing
30 cm (1 ft) between rows

Time to Harvest
40–45 weeks

Recommended Varieties
Radar (white), Red Cross (red)

Advantages
Good use of winter bed space, excellent storing qualities

Disadvantages
Very cheap to buy in the shops

Top Tip
Onions grow into the space they've got, so for bigger
onions leave more space between each bulb

Parsnips

Parsnips had proven tricky germinators for me until the
day Mum swapped tips with 'the woman that does my
feet'. Now, I'm not that well versed with Mum's feet or
their respective ailments, but I think she was talking about
her trip to the local chiropodist.

According to Mum, during one of her visits the
chiropodist said she chits her parsnips to ensure good
germination. This involves sprinkling the seeds onto a damp
piece of kitchen roll laid inside a cling film-covered plastic
tub, which is then popped into an airing cupboard. At the
first sign of germination, the chitting chiropodist whisks the
seeds away and sows them in a toilet roll middle, cut in half
and filled with multipurpose compost. Once the seedling is
4–5 cm (nearly an inch) high, the whole thing (roll and all)
is planted out. The cardboard tube
rots down into the soil, leaving the
parsnip to grow on and hopefully
swell into a chunky prizewinner.

We tried this and germination was
greatly improved, especially as we laid
out more seeds on the paper than we
needed. The cardboard does indeed rot
down a treat, but if like me you haven't
got enough at home and go hunting for
leftovers in the toilets at work, be prepared
for a few funny looks.

Like carrots, stones can split parsnips and hinder their growth, so make sure the soil is fine and well prepared, or consider growing in containers of your own stone-free soil.

Parsnips are slow to reach maturity, but the roots can be left in the ground during winter, and benefit from a sharp frost to sweeten the plant.

When to Sow
February to May

Spacing
Allow 30 cm (1 ft) between each row

Time to Harvest
32–36 weeks

Recommended Varieties
Gladiator, Tender and True

Advantages
Slow to reach maturity, so can be planted alongside a quick cropper such as radish for maximum use of space; can be left in the ground over winter

Disadvantages
Cheap to buy in the shops, not very versatile in the kitchen

Top Tip
Wait until after the first frosts to harvest. The sharp cold releases sugars in the root, which makes for a sweeter taste

Potatoes

Potatoes are easy to grow and produce big yields, making them a staple on most allotments. The average person in the UK feasts on over 100 kilos or 220 pounds of spuds a year, and with more than eighty varieties available to buy in the shops, potatoes are a fun crop to grow as well as harvest. I love digging up potatoes; it's a moment full of anticipation and reminds me of treasure hunts in the garden as a kid, burrowing through the soil looking for prizes. If you've got kids, harvesting spuds is a super way of getting them excited about the allotment.

Potatoes are normally split into earlies and maincrop. Earlies are lifted in summer as small 'new' potatoes, while maincrop are typically dug up in late summer/early autumn for storing into winter. Harvest new potatoes when the plants are in full flower, and maincrop potatoes when the plants turn brown and die off.

Maincrop potatoes take up a lot of space and are very cheap to buy in the shops (local farm shops will often sell big bags of their harvests for as little as a fiver). New potatoes are more expensive and a small row can be beneficial, as the potatoes will be out of the ground in time to re-use the space for a follow-on crop later in the summer.

Buy potatoes in the form of tubers, and plant them with the shoots pointing up, about 15 cm (6 in) deep. Once shoots grow to approximately 20 cm (8 in) high, cover the shoots with earth to within a few centimetres of their tips. Early potatoes are susceptible to frost, so this will protect them. Do this once more a fortnight or so later. This 'earthing up' means that there is more soil around the stalks for the tubers to grow in, and prevents sunlight turning your spuds green and possibly poisonous.

If you don't want to give valuable bed space over to potatoes, try growing some new potatoes in old compost bags. Fill a 6- or 8-litre bag with a mixture of soil and multipurpose or kitchen compost, and plant a tuber in each bag. Keep well watered, as the soil will dry out quicker in bags. Car tyres, three or four high, are also good for growing potatoes.

When to Plant
March for earlies, April for maincrop

Spacing
Keep rows about 75 cm (30 in) apart, with 30 cm (1 ft) between each tuber

Time to Harvest
12–14 weeks for earlies, 19–21 weeks for maincrop

Recommended Varieties
King Edward is a long-standing traditional maincrop, while International Kidney is the variety used to grow the famous Jersey Royal. The wonderfully knobbly Pink Fir Apple is a prolific cropper with excellent storing qualities, while the reliable Sarpo Mira has been bred for maximum blight resistance. Golden Wonder makes perfect chips, or try Desiree for your mash and Ambo for your bakers

Advantages
Prolific cropper, easy to grow, stores well into winter, versatile in the kitchen

Disadvantages
Requires a lot of space, cheap as chips to buy

Top Tip
Sow some quick-cropping salad leaves or radishes in between rows for a handy harvest while waiting for the potatoes to grow

Purple Sprouting Broccoli

Sown in spring to harvest the following year, PSB has a very long growing period, meaning the area set aside for your plants is tied up for a whole year. The plants are also very big, and with a family likely to require two to three plants for a good harvest, those with a small space struggle to justify them.

However, PSB is a strong cropper and the masses of delicious, purple heads help fill the Hungry Gap. Also, early varieties such as the marvellously named Rudolph are now available, cropping from January onwards.

Being a slow grower, you can try maximizing the space by intercropping other smaller, faster growing vegetables in between the plants, like lettuce, spring onions, onions or garlic.

Sow seeds in pots from March to June at a depth of 1–2 cm (less than an inch), and transplant to the veg beds once the seedlings are 20 cm (8 in) high, 60 cm (2 ft) apart. Plant deeply and push soil down firmly around the base to give solid support. Consider staking on exposed sites.

When to Sow
March to June

Spacing
60 cm (2 ft) between rows

Time to Harvest
40+ weeks

Recommended Varieties
Rudolph for early harvests from January, Redhead

Advantages
Crops during the Hungry Gap, other crops can be grown around the plants to maximize space

Disadvantages
Long growing season, takes up a lot of space

Top Tip
Harvest before the flowers open to prolong cropping – regular picking will encourage more shoots to be produced

Radish

One of the advantages of keeping a money-saving spreadsheet is that you can tally the sowing date of a seed against when you first enjoyed a harvest. As a self-confessed veg-by-spreadsheet geek, you can imagine my excitement when I first spotted that a sowing of rapid radishes had gone from seed to plate in four weeks!

Radishes won't save you much money, but in a world where some plants can take months and months to bear goodies, radishes are a cracking choice for anyone looking for a quick veggie fix. Being such speedy croppers, radishes are also excellent for sowing in between slowcoach plants such as brassicas to get a double harvest from one space.

Sow 1–2 cm (less than an inch) deep, and water regularly to ensure a decent root. Small sowings every fortnight will ensure a regular and steady supply.

When to Sow
February to August

Spacing
Allow 10 cm (4 in) between each row

Time to Harvest
3–4 weeks

Recommended Varieties
French Breakfast, Sparkler, Scarlet Globe

Advantages
Very quick to crop, can be 'intercropped' with slow-growing plants for a bonus harvest in small spaces

Disadvantages
Very cheap to buy in the shops, not very versatile in the kitchen

Top Tip
Slice finely and mix with soft cheese and chive for a tasty sandwich spread

Runner Beans

There is a reason why homegrown fruit and veg always taste better than the shop-bought equivalent, and I soon learned that this has a lot to do with harvesting opportunities. Being in control of when you harvest gives a grower the chance to pick crops when they are at their absolute best.

Runner beans are the perfect example of this. The pods can grow more than 50 cm (20 in) in length (my record is 54 cm or 31 in – I really should have entered the allotment show with that beauty), but if you let them grow much more than half this size the beans become stringy and chewy. Get them in the kitchen at about 20 cm (8 in) long and they'll be the best runner beans you've ever tasted.

Runner beans require very rich soil, but can reward you with huge harvests that will last well into autumn. Improve the soil before sowing by digging in well-rotted manure during the winter so you are ready to sow from late May to July. Indoor runners can be sown in pots in April for transplanting later on.

Some traditional climbing varieties can reach 2 metres or 6.5 feet in height, so creating a good support is vital – as is a stool for harvesting. A popular method is to grow them up a wigwam made of bamboo canes, which is also a good way of using space. Insert six to eight canes in the ground and sow a seed 5 cm (2 in) deep either side of each cane. This will boost germination chances and if both seeds do come through they will happily share a cane to wind up.

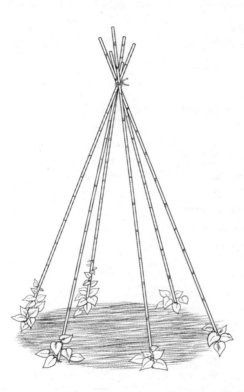

If starting in pots, sow at a similar depth and plant outside when seedlings are 15–20 cm (6–8 in) high and risk of frost has passed. Plant either side of the cane for more vines and a bigger yield.

Like French beans, runners are rapid growers once they get going, so harvest every couple of days if you can in order to get the beans at their tastiest and sweetest. Chop any gluts into chunks about 5 cm (2 in) long and blanche in boiling water before freezing.

When to Sow
April indoors, May to July outside

71

Spacing
25 cm (10 in)

Time to Harvest
12–16 weeks

Recommended Varieties
Scarlet Emperor, White Lady

Advantages
Expensive in the shops, high yields, excellent use of space, freeze well

Disadvantages
Can be fussy if the soil isn't rich enough

Top Tip
Watch out for blackfly. Spray off with warm, soapy water before infestations take hold

Spinach (Perpetual)

There are plenty of glamorous fruits and veg to grow on an allotment, such as tomatoes and strawberries, but sometimes you've got to stand back and admire the underdog. Harvesting the eternally hardy perpetual spinach on a wet, freezing, windy winter's day will be one of those times.

Perpetual spinach is actually a type of chard, but is very closely related to normal spinach. However, it provides an excellent alternative to spinach that, play your cards right, is harvestable all through the year. The plants are cut-and-come-again, and direct sowings in spring and late summer will provide a continuity of leaves, making it a vital crop for the keen money-saver.

The leaves are also very flexible in the kitchen. You can

fold them into all sorts of recipes where it isn't required but tastes great, and they up your five-a-day count with no fuss whatsoever. Try perpetual spinach in curries, tarts, pasta and quiches or on pizza for a hit of covert healthiness.

Sowing and growing couldn't be simpler: sow in rows 3 cm (1 in) deep, and thin out to 20 cm (8 in) apart later on. If germination is patchy, transplant bunched seedlings to bare patches and water in well. Harvest when the leaves are about 20 cm (8 in) long for the best flavour and texture, cutting the stems at the base. The stems can also be eaten, and are a nice addition to stir-fries.

When to Sow
March to August

Spacing
45 cm (18 in) between rows

Time to Harvest
10–12 weeks

Recommended Varieties
Perpetual spinach is actually a variety of chard. Try Bright Lights for more colour

Advantages
Heavy croppers, long harvest, easy to grow, reliable, hardy, cut-and-come-again, versatile in the kitchen. If only all crops were like perpetual spinach ...

Disadvantages
Let me know if you find any!

Top Tip
Perpetual spinach doesn't mind drier soils, so is an excellent choice for a container if you're squeezed for space

Spring Greens

January and February are tough months on an allotment plot or vegetable patch. There is little to harvest, the stores will be beginning to run dry and the weather is uninspiring. One veg that always cheers me up during this period is the good old spring green, a cabbage variety that will stand through winter and provide thick, tasty and nutritious leaves when fresh options are at a premium.

A spring green is a cabbage used for the leaves, before the middle 'hearts up', that is, forms a firm head. Cabbage varieties specifically for use as a spring green exist, such as Greensleeves, but I find summer varieties planted late and overwintered provide bigger plants and better harvests. Hispi has proven reliable for me, as has the winter cabbage variety January King.

Sowings in July and August will deliver post-Christmas harvests, which will last through the Hungry Gap (the period between the last of the winter veg and the first of the spring harvest) and into late spring. Spreading harvests as evenly across the year as you can is important for saving money, so anything harvestable at the turn of a new year is worth its weight in gold.

Sow seeds directly or in pots 1 cm (half an inch) deep. Thin to 36 cm (14 in) apart, or plant out to a similar distance if transplanting from pots.

When to Sow
July–August for harvesting from January onwards

Spacing
30 cm (1 ft) between rows

Time to Harvest
20–35 weeks

Recommended Varieties
Hispi, Greensleeves, Duncan

Advantages
Provide a harvest during winter, can leave in the ground during winter and harvest when you need them

Disadvantages
Susceptible to cabbage white butterflies

Top Tip
Net your plants until winter if the season has been particularly bad for cabbage whites

Squashes

In the world of growing vegetables to save money, the squash is a Big Gun. Expensive in the shops, a ridiculously long storage life (I've eaten Crown Prince varieties in June of the following year), and as long as your soil is well manured and the plants are well watered, they're a cinch to grow.

What's more, squashes of any variety are brilliantly versatile in the kitchen, lending themselves to curries, risottos, pasties, pies, soup, lasagnes, pizza and even cakes. You can slice a butternut in half and stuff it, and they'll even make a side dish in the form of mash or chips. What's more, an average size squash will comfortably contribute to two separate meals. Bang for buck, squashes rule the beds.

They're a gorgeous-looking crop, too. Crown Prince is a lovely, duck egg colour, while Turk's Turban is a real allotment head-turner and quite possibly the craziest looking veg you can grow. The only downside is that they do take up a lot of space, but a healthy plant will yield three to four fruits.

Sow in May in pots of multipurpose compost, 2 cm (nearly an inch) deep, and transplant out once the risk of frost has passed. Squash plants like full sun and rich soil, so dig a little pit and toss in a mixture of well-rotted manure and the soil you've removed before planting. Mound up around the squash so that water stays in and around the base of the plant when you water.

Harvest at the beginning of autumn, before the weather turns wetter. Leave to dry in the sun before storing in a cool, dark place like a shed, garage or cupboard under the stairs.

Invest big savings in the best quality vegetable peeler you can find. It'll make taking the skin off so much easier!

When to Sow
April to May

Spacing
Minimum of 1 m (3–4 ft) between plants

Time to Harvest
15–20 weeks

Recommended Varieties
Butternut varieties such as Harrier and Hunter for ease
of use in the kitchen, Crown Prince for storing longevity,
Turk's Turban for fun

Advantages
Expensive to buy, versatile in the kitchen, easy to grow,
big yields, will store for months

Disadvantages
Take up a lot of space

Top Tip
Squash plants grow very large, so put a tall stick in the
ground next to the base. This will make it much easier to
finding the roots when watering after the plants start to
sprawl

Sweetcorn

Like tomatoes, sweetcorn is a plant to grow
for taste. It is important to get a cob to
plate as soon as possible as the sugars
start turning starchy immediately after
picking, and the flavour becomes
compromised. However, a quick,
sharp harvest and cook combo rewards
growers with the most incredibly sweet-
tasting vegetable that could almost
be dessert rather than dinner.

The bad news is that unlike
tomatoes, each plant doesn't provide
much return for the large amount of space
required. Sweetcorn is best grown in blocks,
and with each plant only yielding two or

three cobs, it can easily take up a whole bed. With three locally grown cobs often available from greengrocers for a pound, sweetcorn is a bit of a luxury on a small plot – but my, what a luxury it is. In fact, if you can find room for some sweetcorn on your plot, it is worth growing a cob just for a sumptuous August allotment barbecue.

Sow in April or May indoors in pots, and plant out after the last frosts. Choose a sunny, sheltered spot, and plant out in blocks, 45 cm (18 in) apart.

When the tasselly ends are dying off, check to see if a cob is ready to harvest. Peel back the outer skin (the husk), and pierce a grain with your fingernail. If the juice comes out milky, the cob is ripe.

When to Sow
April and May

Spacing
In blocks, 45 cm (18 in) apart

Time to Harvest
12–18 weeks

Recommended Varieties
Swift, Mirai

Advantages
Far sweeter and tastier than shop-bought cobs

Disadvantages
Space-hungry, cheap to buy

Top Tip
For the sweetest cobs, choose 'supersweet' varieties

Tomatoes

If you ever needed convincing that your own food dramatically outstrips the taste of shop-bought alternatives, then toms are the crop to do it. Tomatoes are like sweets, and there is a divine taste to homegrown toms freshly picked from the plot that can't be matched. They happen to be expensive in the shops, too, but that's irrelevant where tomatoes are concerned. They're just too amazing not to grow.

Broadly speaking, there are three types of tomato to grow: the big fat beefsteaks, little sweet cherry toms and a generic, heavy cropping 'normal' tom.

Beefsteaks can grow to a whopping size without losing flavour and slice easily, while cherry tomatoes are excellent in salads and suitable for growing in containers or hanging baskets.

Tomatoes are heat-loving plants, so sow undercover in pots in mid- to late spring, and make sure the frosts are well gone before planting out. Choose a sheltered, sunny spot and, like squashes and courgettes, dig manure in and plant in a recess.

Remember to water often, as tomatoes are thirsty plants. Consistency is also important with tomatoes, so try to give the plants a good watering at least three times a week during summer.

A fully laden tomato plant can be really heavy, so tie the main stem to a bamboo cane for support. The stems are quite soft, though, so don't tie the string too tight or it will dig into the plant.

Also, remember to pinch out side shoots, as these will grow perpetually and take energy away from the main stem. If you're unsure of what a sideshoot looks like, the best way I've heard them described is to stand on your head, and imagine something growing out of your armpits.

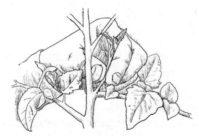

Standing on your head is optional – just picturing it will help identify the bit of a tomato that you nip out.

When to Sow
March to May

Spacing
60 cm (2 ft) between plants. Decent spacing is important so that moisture does not build up around the plant. This causes blight, which can wreck a crop

Time to Harvest
16–20 weeks

Recommended Varieties
Marmande for beefsteaks, Gardener's Delight or Moneymaker for reliability, Tumbling Toms for containers

Advantages
Very expensive in the shops, heavy crops, versatile in the kitchen, delicious!

Disadvantages
Too many plants can easily lead to a glut. Cooking and freezing passata is a good way of keeping tomatoes for use in winter cooking

Top Tip
For the very best flavour and juiciest texture, leave a tomato on the vine until it is deep red in colour

Herbs

One of the most exciting and rewarding challenges of running an allotment is cooking around what you're harvesting. Herbs have a big part to play in pepping up dishes and turning your well-earned harvests into culinary delights, whether you're sprinkling basil into pasta, sage into a risotto or mint on your spuds.

You won't save much from growing herbs, but wastage is reduced since you won't have to buy oversized bags of pre-chopped herbs just for one dish. The convenience of having a selection at hand is also a big bonus when looking to add flavour to a meal. For that reason, I'd recommend growing your herbs in the garden rather than the allotment, so you can quickly pop out and harvest a handful of flavour. Consider positioning the bed near to the back door, as herbs are very decorative, and make a lovely view out of a kitchen window. What's more, no one enjoys trudging to the end of the garden in the middle of winter for a handful of sage leaves.

Herbs are also suitable for containers, so if you've only got a courtyard or balcony, a herb garden is still possible.

Herbs are split into annuals, that die off after one year, and perennials, that grow back again in the spring. Once you've got the basics right in your herb bed, the plants are very easy to grow and require little maintenance. Some actually grow a little too well, and will dominate a bed. Mint and sage will take over and dwarf some of the smaller herbs, and mint roots will very quickly multiply right across beds. I now grow my mints exclusively in pots after a particularly prolific spearmint plant went ballistic and grew to the size of a small bush immediately outside my patio doors. I lost hours of my life one winter trying to eek out every single little piece of root, before they rejuvenated and started penning us in again …

To start a herb bed, find a sunny spot that drains well. If your soil is heavy or holds water, consider building a raised bed or using containers. Add some goodness to the soil, but don't make it too rich. Well-rotted manure is a little too potent, but leaf mould or garden compost is just the job.

Herbs are best bought as plants or root divisions and planted directly, but if you're on a budget they are easy to grow from seed. Also, perennial herbs are easy to multiply, either by taking cuttings or breaking up clumps and replanting, so after you've invested in a plant once, you shouldn't have to buy one again. If you're lucky, a fellow grower will let you take some cuttings or root divisions, especially with the fast-growing, dominant varieties like mint, rosemary and sage.

Popular Annual Herbs

Basil

I enjoy growing basil next to my tomatoes, as there is no better match in allotment cooking than these two summer delights. Basil is a tender plant, so grows better and for longer with some protection. A greenhouse is obviously the best choice, but a sheltered, sunny spot will also yield some healthy leaves, as will a warm windowsill.

Sow indoors in spring, in pots, and plant out once the risk of frost has passed. If you do have some cover, sow again in high summer for a later crop. Nip off the tips before they flower to increase the longevity of the plant.

Coriander

Ideal for adding to curries, soups and salads, coriander is hardier than basil but still requires a sunny spot for good growth.

Sow coriander directly, 1 cm (½ in) deep, from April, and thin seedlings to one every 20–30 cm (8–12 in). If you've got a greenhouse or even a cloche, coriander can be sown in late summer for use in the winter.

Parsley

Strictly speaking, parsley is actually a biennial, which means you will need to replace the plant after the second season, when it will go to flower. Flat-leafed varieties are stronger in flavour than their curly counterparts.

Sow in pots or direct between April and July, and then again under cover from August onwards for a winter supply. Parsley can also be grown in a pot indoors on a sunny windowsill.

Popular Perennial Herbs

Chives

Chives are normally used to add an onion flavour to salads, soups, quiches and other savoury dishes, and are easily grown in pots or from seeds sown straight into the ground. The plant is low-maintenance and will tolerate some shade, making chives a great choice for that troublesome corner where nothing else will grow. The pink flowers make a lovely display, too, and help attract bees to your plot.

Sow seeds in pots or prepared beds from March until June. If sowing in pots, sow three to five in each pot and plant out as a whole once the frosts have passed. Divide clumps into new plants in autumn, and keep one clump in a pot for indoor use through winter.

Mint

Mint spreads incredibly fast and will take over a whole bed in a summer if you let it. To prevent this, buy as divided roots or plants, and plant in containers or large sunken pots.

There are lots of mint varieties to try, but the most popular are apple mint and spearmint.

Oregano and Marjoram

Sweet-smelling oregano – and its close relative marjoram – is often used on meat. Sow inside in pots from February to June, and plant out when risk of frost has passed. Oregano is not as invasive as mint, but still requires some control so cut back during winter ready for spring regrowth. Leaves can be dried for winter use.

Sage

Another herb regularly used on meats, sage can also spruce up many other dishes, such as risotto and quiches. Sage is hardy, so is normally available for picking most of the year round, but can grow very large and dominant so keep in check by cutting away older, woodier stems in spring.

Sow inside from March to May in pots and plant out once risk of frost has passed. Sage is very low-maintenance once established. Try the Tricolor variety for added attractiveness in the herb garden.

Take cuttings from soft, younger stems in summer to propagate more plants.

Thyme

A pretty and delicate plant, thyme is a pungent herb used regularly on meats. Sow in pots or a seed tray indoors from February to April, and plant out once risk of frost has passed. Thyme is drought-tolerant and won't sulk in poorer soil, making it a great use of a dodgy spot on your plot or in the garden.

Like sage, take cuttings from soft, younger stems in summer to propagate more plants.

Fruit

Fruit is one of the most joyous things to grow on an allotment. From the beautifully sugary scent of the first spring rhubarb, to the succulent sweetness of a juicy strawberry and the bonus of autumn-fruiting raspberry harvests, fruit adds a real sense of luxury to any veg plot or kitchen garden.

A lot of fruit is also very expensive in the shops. Soft

fruit commands heady prices, even in season. Even the cheapest of supermarket strawbs will fetch a fiver a kilo, while just a small tub of raspberries can leave you £2 lighter. Not only is fresh allotment fruit delicious, it will also save you a bag full of cash.

If you're growing with that in mind, it is worth sticking to a few crowns of rhubarb and the simple soft fruits rather than splashing out on expensive trees. Plums, apples, pears and greengages are all wonderful additions to a plot, but decent trees will put a big hole in your pocket and take a good few years before they start providing solid harvests and save you money. They're definitely for the long term, whereas strawberries, rhubarb, raspberries and gooseberries will yield harvests almost straightaway, and improve year on year.

Plums and apples are often found for free in parks and open scrubland, or can be picked up for a song outside people's houses. With that in mind, I'd definitely recommend keeping fruit simple, and concentrating on the following common allotment treats. As well as being high value, these fruits are low-maintenance, easy to grow, quickly productive and cash-friendly to buy and multiply.

Soft fruit needs protection from frosts and chilly conditions, so lend the plants a hand by choosing sunny spots for planting, well away from any frost pockets. A sunny location is also vital to help the fruit ripen properly. Unlike most vegetables, fruits tend to be perennial and are therefore considered permanent once in the ground. Although plants will tolerate the odd move, try to choose a good location first time round and stick to it.

If you do find you've made a mistake and your plants are sulking in their new home, don't fret. I'm a terrible tinkerer and always thinking of completely redesigning my plot. I've moved lots of fruit and generally they'll forgive you by the time the following year comes around. Wherever the plants end up, make sure you add plenty of organic matter into the soil and water regularly.

Blackberries

With blackberries so readily available a short walk from many people's houses in the UK, you can quite fairly ask yourself why anyone would bother wasting precious plot space growing cultivated varieties.

Once upon a time, this was definitely at odds with my inner being. That kind of dreamy hunter-gatherer that lurks in most men had decided that growing a cultivated variety of the blackberry was somehow conflicting with nature. I was a blackberry purist, and wasn't for budging. Then one day a good friend bought me a couple of plants as a present. I was grateful, of course, but I couldn't help thinking I wouldn't be giving valuable growing space over to them. However, like all growers, I hate seeing lonely plants sat in pots rather than out in the soil, so we found some room on the plot.

What followed was nothing short of a revelation. The fruits were sweeter, plumper and far more abundant than anything I'd previously found in the hedgerow. I became a cultivated convert, and I still am.

Blackberries trail, so can be trained upwards to save space. If your plot is exposed, you can also train them on wires tied to posts to create an edible windbreak, which will not only provide tasty fruit but also help protect more delicate plants from the elements.

The fruit freezes well, too. Pop excess harvests straight into freezer bags for use later.

Raspberries

The raspberry harvest can be extended by growing summer-fruiting varieties together with varieties that crop in autumn. Summer varieties will yield fruit from June onwards, with autumn varieties arriving in August. They will continue to crop until the first frosts of winter.

However, if space is tight, consider growing just autumn-fruiting varieties rather than their summer equivalents. Generally speaking, autumn varieties are more productive and the fruits bigger. Polka and Autumn Bliss are excellent choices.

Like most soft fruits, raspberries are expensive in the shops and although canes can be pricey initially, you can take new canes from old to increase your stock. Raspberries will tolerate some shade, but they do appreciate healthy, rich soil so dig in plenty of compost or well-rotted manure before planting.

For summer-fruiting raspberries, cut back the canes to the ground straight after harvesting, and do the same for autumn-fruiters in February. For both, add a mulch of compost or manure around the base of the canes in spring.

Rhubarb

Although strictly speaking a vegetable, rhubarb is used as a fruit and flies the flag as the first 'fruit' of the season. Rhubarb crowns can be 'forced' into producing a crop as early as February by putting a bucket over the top; otherwise crops will be ready from late March and will continue producing until mid-summer.

Rhubarb is the ultimate low-maintenance perennial, so is perfect for a money-conscious plot holder looking for maximum return on investment and time. The sugary stems that arrive in spring after a winter of greens and brassicas are magical, and I find the first rhubarb harvest a wonderfully symbolic moment of seasonal change.

Rhubarb enjoys life in rich soil, so make sure there is a good amount of well-rotted manure dug in before planting out crowns. Also, dump a couple of spades full of manure around your crowns every autumn to replenish the crowns and help boost yields the following spring.

Excess stalks can be cut into inch-long chunks and frozen for stewing in winter.

Strawberries

A steady supply of strawberries should definitely be a plot priority, and not just for the money-saving. Strawberries are another expensive soft fruit to buy, but they're also one of the tastiest crops to grow yourself, and having control of your harvest means you can pick the fruits when they are at their reddest and most delicious.

Strawberries are reliable and easy to grow, providing excellent harvests for the space they're given. Plants are inexpensive, and are best planted one year for cropping the next. When preparing a bed for planting, make sure lots of organic matter is dug in beforehand, and plant out in autumn or mid-spring. The plants can be positioned fairly close together, and don't necessarily have to be in neat and tidy rows.

Water regularly once fruits begin to form, but make sure the soil doesn't get too wet, as the fruits will rot. Spreading straw underneath the plants will help keep them off the ground and also stops rotting after heavy rain showers. The last thing you want after waiting all winter for lovely summer fruits is soggy strawbs, so keep on the ball with harvesting.

The rough texture of the straw will also help keep slugs and snails off your prized crops. They love strawberries as much as the rest of us, and often it is a race with the slimies to the perfect strawberry. But they don't like the coarseness of straw so lay some down and give yourself a head start.

Use the straw to suppress weeds, too, but if any do come through pull them out gently by hand as strawberry roots are shallow and easily disturbed.

Strawberry plants will need replacing every three or four years, but this is easily and cheaply done. During the summer, the plants will send out 'runners', which self-root in the soil. Simply find the pincer-looking roots from the runners and pot them up in multipurpose compost. Place a stone on top of the root if it won't sit tight in the compost. Once the root has established, cut the runner away from the original plant and keep the strawberry plant for planting out in autumn.

CHAPTER 4

Plot Planning

Deciding What to Grow

As I write, there is a bunch of parsnips at the bottom of my fridge. They've been there for two weeks. I don't dislike parsnips, but we don't roast much in my house. Parsnips are a bit of a Christmas thing for us.

These parsnips, past their best and now probably destined for a soup or the compost, remind me of something important and particularly pertinent to the veg grower looking to save money: don't be tempted by every seed under the sun – grow what you eat.

On the face of it, this is an obvious tip, but it is an often-overlooked one (see my parsnips above). If you eat a lot of a certain fruit or vegetable, it makes sense to grow as much of it as you can. If you only eat a couple of cauliflowers a year, I'd recommend buying them and concentrating on growing the crops that you and your family eat lots of instead.

The annual seed-buying trip to the garden centre is full of temptation, and it is very easy for the exhilaration of the new growing season to grab hold of you. Before you know it, your basket is full of seeds, so try to make a list of what you intend to grow prior to visiting. This will help focus the mind and ensure you don't rack up a £50 bill!

As well as growing fruit and vegetables that you and your family eat regularly, there are other factors to bear in mind when trying to save money.

Next time you visit the supermarket, make a note of the most expensive produce. Some vegetables, such as onions and potatoes, are so cheap to buy and so readily available that there isn't much of a financial case for growing them. On the other hand, vegetables such as tomatoes, leeks and butternut squashes command high prices, so finding space on your plot for these vegetables is well worth it. A packet of leek seeds will cost between £1 and £2, and just two rows could easily be worth £50 once you've harvested all the shanks.

Soft fruit is also very expensive in the shops. Although there is an initial outlay, summer favourites such as strawberries are easy to grow, and it is easy to propagate more plants and bushes from your existing ones for free.

The space that a plant takes up is also worth considering, especially if your growing area is small. Could you use that space more wisely? Globe artichokes, for example, look beautiful on an allotment plot and are expensive to buy, but they take up huge amounts of space. The return from two plants when compared to a block of dwarf French beans would be minimal.

Reliability is also important when you're growing to save money – the last thing the cash-conscious grower wants is a failed crop. All growing environments are different, so only time will help you work out which plants are particularly prone to different diseases and pests, and gradually you will be able to decide what gives you the best chance of a successful and plentiful harvest.

Sweet potato is renowned as being a very tricky vegetable to grow in the UK, even though the tubers are now readily available to buy; cauliflowers can be fussy and require lots of attention; and broad beans are notorious for being wiped out by blackfly. If this is your first season of growing, consider sticking to easier crops, such as courgettes, beetroots, leeks and French beans, to ensure a solid, money-saving year.

When you're buying seeds, check the packets for cropping times. Quick croppers, such as salad and radishes, are very efficient users of space, as they can be turned around quickly and can be planted as an 'intercrop' while you wait for the main plant to grow. A good example of this is planting salad leaves on the side of potato mounds. By the time the potatoes pop up and take over, the salad leaves will have finished, giving you a bonus crop from a single space.

Try to think beyond the immediate harvest, too. Not all fruit and veg has to be eaten there and then. Many legumes, such as peas, mangetout, runner, broad and French beans, freeze well and properly stored squashes and potatoes can last all through the winter.

Similarly, plan for winter. Frozen and stored crops are excellent contributors in the colder months, but nothing beats freshly harvested produce. Make sure your plot is a balance between the bounty of summer and the steady, reliable winter greens like chard, leeks and kale. A steady stream of available harvests are much better for the bank account than summer gluts that the gardener can't keep up with.

Winter greens also boast long harvesting periods – sometimes as long as nine months in the case of cut-and-come-again varieties like chard and kale. When there isn't much else coming off the plot during January and February, I'm always really grateful for these dependable and consistent vegetables, especially as the more you pick, the more they'll crop.

A fruit or vegetable has to be useful as well. Versatility in the kitchen means that one harvest might contribute to two or three meals during the course of the week. Squashes are the kings of the kitchen, and can be used in all sorts of tasty dishes, including curries, risottos, soup, mash, lasagnes, pies and even cakes. One decent-sized squash can easily help feed a family for two evenings.

It is worth weighing up the various pluses and minuses of each vegetable before committing to growing it. For example, purple sprouting broccoli takes up a lot of space and has a very long growing period, but it can provide fresh crops from January to April, when there is little else to harvest. This planning helps prioritize the good-value plants and is particularly worth doing if you're limited in space. If you're looking to save money, allow no room for passengers!

Of course, this is all an excellent guide for helping decide what to grow, but ultimately taste is just as important. Saving money, ensuring efficient use of space and achieving high levels of productivity are all noble motives for growing your own, but for many allotment holders, taste is still king. Homegrown crops, harvested fresh from the plant, will be the most delicious fruit and vegetables you'll taste, easily surpassing shop-bought equivalents. Over time, you'll work out the varieties that leave you licking your lips and these should always find a place on your plot.

Sweetcorn was the first vegetable to teach me that finding room for something grand is a must. The first cobs we grew ourselves were so incredibly sweet that they could easily have been a dessert rather than an accompaniment to our barbeque. Sweetcorn plants take up a lot of space, so the yields are low when compared to most other crops, but boy, are they worth that space! Even if you are growing specifically to reduce bills, it's nice to throw off the money-saving, crop-maximizing shackles and stick in a few luxuries. After my sweetcorn experience, there will always be a place on my patch for a few of those succulent cobs.

Producing a Plot Plan

You've decided what plants you're going to grow and where you're going to grow them – now it is the time to get planning properly. I love producing my plot plan. I normally do this after Christmas, when I find myself feeling particularly energized by the turn of the new year, and it has become somewhat of a ritual in my growing year. I recommend a cold winter's night, a mug of steaming tea and a fresh notebook, although I enjoy the annual excitement of a plot plan so much that I've experimented with a number of different ways of making one.

My most artistic attempt so far has been a scale drawing, complete with colour-coded beds and plants. I commandeered a surveyor's wheel to get the right sizes and went to town with a set of coloured pencils on graph paper. I got a few odd stares as I pushed the wheel around my beds, but it meant I could plan pretty accurately how many plants I could squeeze in. If you know your plot's size, there are also plot planners available on the web that will help you design your plot and calculate for you the number of plants required. Some work month by month, showing spaces created by finished plants, which allows you to plan successional sowings all through the year. For a small monthly fee, premium planners will even create a planting plan adapted to your own regional climate and set up email reminders in case you're the forgetful type.

Here are some of the most important things to consider when designing your plot.

Crop Rotation

When deciding what plants to put where, try grouping the legume, brassica and root veg families together, as they will all have similar growing requirements, which makes soil preparation easier. These three groups also form the basis of an easy crop rotation sequence. Crop rotation is simply ensuring that similar plants are not planted in the same place two years running, which is done for two main reasons: to disrupt the life cycle of pests and diseases associated with each crop, and to help prevent the soil breaking down from excessive demand for specific nutrients when the same plants are planted in the same place year after year.

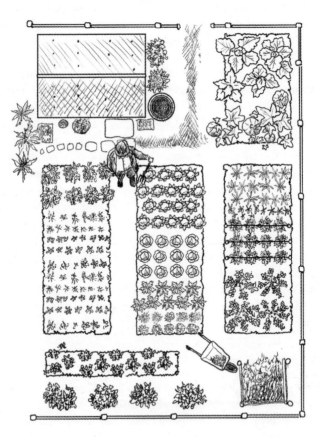

The main families are: legumes, which are crops with pods, such as peas, broad beans, runner beans and French beans, while brassicas are essentially anything cabbagey. This includes leafy winter greens such as kale, as well as sprouts, broccoli and cauliflowers. Root veg are potatoes, beetroot, carrots, parsnips, swedes, turnips and radishes.

The most basic form of crop rotation is remembering not to put plants in the same spot the following year, but that takes a darn good memory and a big notebook! The easiest system is to include three vegetable beds in your plot plan – one for each family – and rotate the legumes, brassicas and root crops around each year. Grow onions, leeks and garlic in with the legumes, as they enjoy the same soil. Squashes, courgettes, tomatoes and cucumbers can be grown with any of the plant families but take a lot out of the soil, so make sure you add plenty of organic matter during winter to replenish nutrients.

Space and Access

When deciding what to put where, make sure there is plenty of space between plants and rows. Some online plot planners will automatically do this for you, but it is an easy mistake to try and shoehorn in every vegetable plant seed under the sun (plus a few more). Planting too close together can restrict growth and air circulation (which encourages blight) and spread disease between crops. Giving plants space to breathe is important, and two well-spaced plants will often give just as much yield as four crammed close together.

Space is also significant when considering where to stand when harvesting and watering. During my first year of growing vegetables in my back garden, I set aside one single space and filled it with plants willy-nilly. It looked great in spring, with plants neatly spread across the bed, but as they grew bigger and closer together I soon found out it is very easy to wipe out a whole plant with one awkward stumble. Furthermore, actually manoeuvring around the plot required a litheness more akin to a seasoned yoga instructor than a peculiarly shaped man who can't touch his toes.

Distinct paths on your plot can help make sure it is easy to get around, keep your precious plants from getting squashed by a size 9 boot, and provide boundaries between beds. Grass paths are common but obviously require cutting and edging so that they don't encroach on beds. At home, I've skimmed off the top of the turf and covered it with weed-suppressant membrane, adding wood chippings on top of that. Paving stones or gravel are more expensive options, but all three are low-maintenance, weatherproof and one less thing to weed.

Shade and Frost

Weather will have a big impact on how well your vegetables grow, and although we can't control how much rain we get or whether the sun shines, there are some steps we can take to give our plants a helping hand. Many plants, particularly early summer types, are susceptible to frost, so identifying and avoiding frost pockets is advisable. Frost can be more prevalent in slopes or behind fences and hedges, and reduces the growing season in that area, so avoid planting out summer veg here if you can. The easiest way of spotting a frost pocket is to wrap up warm and take a trip to your plot first thing on the morning of a light frost, which will show where the pockets are. You might choose to put hardy winter veg there, or avoid the area completely and use it for a bench, shed or wildlife pond.

Shady spots can also be equally problematic. These are easily identified – normally lying next to structures or under trees – and they limit your options for growing. During summer, a cool, shady area is most welcome to the hardworking plot holder, so again, a cosy bench for resting is worth considering. However, some vegetables, such as leafy greens and salads, will tolerate some shade if you do want to cultivate in the area. The best bet might well be rhubarb, however, which doesn't mind shade and, being a perennial, won't require moving from year to year.

Using Raised Beds

Another thing to consider when contemplating your plot is whether you'd like to use raised beds rather than conventional beds straight in the ground. Raised beds are essentially a frame, usually made from wooden planks, set on top of the ground and filled with soil and organic matter.

I began using raised beds when I started my kitchen garden. One of the little-mentioned differences between growing in a garden and on an allotment is that when you grow in your garden, you have to look at it every time you enter the kitchen or hang the washing out. I was looking for a plot that was as aesthetically pleasing as it was productive, and every plot I'd ever seen that used raised beds was very easy on the eye.

There are other more functional advantages of raised beds, too. My raised beds have taught me to be more careful with the spacing, and everything is now neat and ordered. This makes daily jobs like weeding, thinning out and harvesting much easier. My back is thankful that I don't have to lean down so far, I can reach all around without standing on the soil and compacting it down, and the wooden planks around the sides keep the grass from intruding into the soil. All these little elements help make the plot more manageable and free up time to do other things.

One of the biggest advantages of using raised beds is the control they give you over your soil. Raised beds give the grower the chance to choose what type of organic matter and soil goes into them. If you build your own raised beds, you're effectively deciding what type of soil to use from the start and you know how to improve it as time goes on. This is particularly handy should your basic soil be heavy or poor quality. Here in Essex, the soil is predominantly clay, which is heavy and difficult to grow in. Raised beds meant I could start afresh with good quality growing matter, mixing soil elements to my heart's content. My garden beds are now a mixture of topsoil, seaweed, kitchen compost, manure, leaf mould and a few bags of cheap multipurpose compost. The result is a lovely, rich growing medium that has produced some great harvests and matched anything that I've grown on my allotment. I'm pleased to say that the horrible clay is now a thing of the past.

If you're looking to grow fruit or veg that is more demanding than most, or maybe just doesn't like stony soil, you can also install a raised bed with soil to suit that particular crop. A good example would be blueberries, which require an acidic soil to thrive.

There are some downsides to raised beds that are worth noting. Because they drain so well, they may also require more watering, which not only creates extra work, but can also make leaving them tricky when you go off on your summer holiday. Getting hold of materials and soil can be expensive unless you can find some freebie alternatives along the way. Scaffold boards are perfect for building raised beds, as they are hardwearing and sturdy, and because they are replaced regularly for safety reasons, used boards are readily available and fairly cheap. Scaffold boards are also easy to move around and install. I've seen raised beds made from longer-lasting materials such as brick, but they're trickier to build and, once concreted in, are immoveable.

Railways sleepers look beautiful, but are very pricey. Don't be tempted by the cheaper old-style sleepers, as they've been treated with toxic preservatives. Modern wood treatments are considered safe, however, but expect to pay more for this.

The optimum size for raised beds is between 1.2 and 1.5 m (4 to 5 ft) wide, as it's just the right size to be able to lean across without treading on the soil too much. You want to avoid walking on the soil as much as possible, as this can cause compaction.

Building Raised Beds

Clear the area of any weeds etc., and then dig a shallow recess to sit the board in. It doesn't have to be any deeper than a couple of centimetres or an inch or so – just deep enough to help support the board so that it can stand

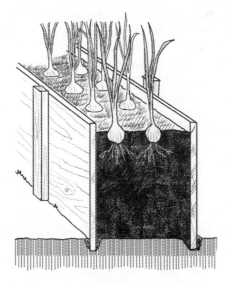

proud. Use a spirit level to check whether it is straight, and add soil underneath the board to even it up if need be. Support the boards by banging stakes into the soil on the outside edges at various points around the bed. The soil will push the boards out tight against the stakes, so that they hold themselves in position. You can also put a square post in each inside corner of your bed for extra support, and nail through the board into the post.

Once you've put your bed together, it's time to fill it with lovely soil and organic matter! Topsoil can be bought from most gardening centres or builders' merchants, but the cost can be offset by sourcing free organic matter such as well-rotted manure, kitchen compost or even seaweed. I also used leaf mould and cheap multipurpose compost to bulk up the soil.

Spread the soil evenly, but watch out, as the soil level will drop over time, so you will need to add some more soil and manure later on. If you are struggling to find cheap or free materials, soil and organic matter, it is important to remember that your soil is a long-term investment, so it is worth spending the money if it means you ultimately have the best conditions for growing your own food. You'll soon be making the cash back in delicious, freshly harvested produce!

CHAPTER 5

Preparing an Overgrown Plot

So, you've pored over seed catalogues, planned your plot and bought your tools. Everything is ready to go and the lighter days cannot come soon enough. Everything is planned meticulously, you're going to be the local allotment king or queen, and your mouth is salivating at the thought of all that stunning, homegrown produce.

Except that there's a spanner in the works. You head down to be shown your new plot and your heart sinks: it's a complete mess – overgrown and unloved, with weeds, nettles, brambles and grass covering every corner. I was lucky with my first plot, as it was being given up by a plot holder who'd decided to scale back after years of growing, so the beds were in great nick. Unfortunately, this is not normally the case, and often there is nothing else on offer but the neglected jungle plot.

This happened to me when I took on an allotment with my mum, and later when I began growing in my garden. Both times, we were faced with clearing chest-high weeds to return the space to somewhere suitable for vegetable beds, but the good news is that this isn't as much of a slog as you might think.

Rotavating

The quickest way to clear a plot is to use a rotavator, a machine with rotating blades that break up the soil. Rotavators can be hired for a day, and if you rip out the big weeds by hand and then rotavate, there is every chance you'll have soil to sow into before the weekend is out. However, the 'R-word' is a contentious one and divides opinion in some gardening circles. The trouble is, a rotavator has a number of downsides. For a start, the machine won't kill off all the weeds. Rotavators cut up the roots and therefore actually multiply perennial weeds such as couch grass and bindweed, so although the soil will be clean for a while, the weeds will eventually come back even more ferociously.

Many believe that there is no quick fix for getting rid of weeds other than digging them out manually, and in doing so a gardener will gain an understanding of the soil they have. Rotavating can also damage soil structure, especially heavy soils such as clay. It often forms a water-resistant barrier, causing poor drainage and preventing roots from growing deep enough.

The traditional approach to removing weeds can be time-consuming and a lot of hard graft, and this slower approach could mean no growing at all for the first year of rent. My local plot committee adopts the rotavator approach on overgrown plots, and this is where I also have sympathies with a rotavator. I hate seeing newcomers quickly giving up on growing veggies since their plots were covered in weeds for the first season and they just couldn't see past this to being able to actually sow seeds. A rotavator, however much of a shortcut, means beginners can get going virtually from day one and begin their journey towards the amazing buzz of harvesting homegrown produce.

Any decision on the use of a rotavator should rest on

how quickly you want a productive plot. That first year is so important for a new grower, as it decides whether they'll continue or not. Spending months toiling away at a weed jungle with no light at the end of the tunnel can kill enthusiasm, yet get a good first summer's harvest and a grower is hooked forever.

'I don't want to use a rotavator'

If you don't want to use a rotavator to get your unruly plot back in line, there are a number of different tactics for clearing efficiently and getting seeds in the ground quickly. I've used the following tips and methods to clear both allotments and my garden, and found that you don't have to graft forever regardless of plot condition.

Little and Often

When undertaking heavy work on the plot, it is worth taking a 'little and often' approach. A whole day of digging and pulling up weeds can be boring and disheartening, especially if you're on your own, and you'll begin to think you're not making any progress. Little and often will help keep your spirits high, as it won't feel like a constant struggle. It is vital that you look forward to going to the plot and don't let things get on top of you. Clearing a plot by hand is hard graft and can cause aches and pains, especially if you're not used to doing it. It is worth breaking up the sessions if possible to ease the impact on muscles.

Know when to call it a day – don't stay on the plot if you don't want to be there. If you yawn, go home and put your feet up!

Being able to see some progress is always a morale-booster, so regularly standing back and admiring spruced-up sections, rather than slogging through hours and hours to cultivate one big section, is much better for the mind. Instead of concentrating on clearing your whole plot ready for one big growing splurge, it's worth considering clearing, digging and preparing small areas with specific plants in mind. This requires some planning, but means that you can grow as you go along, as well as getting parts of your plot producing crops within just a few weeks of taking it on.

On our plot, we sowed in pots at home and then dug over the allotment space while the seedlings grew. This gave us time to prepare a small, manageable chunk of ground for the plants as they grew. I found this to be a good approach, as we were focused on our digging, and there was a clear goal to what we were doing. It also provided motivation when clearing and digging were proving a pain, as we knew that once we'd finished there would be some plants ready to go in.

Raised Beds

There was an overgrown plot next to my old allotment, and the new plot holder pulled the big stuff up and then built raised beds. Any remaining grass was left as paths in between the beds, and very smart it looked, too. My neighbour could start growing immediately, rather than waiting for months while he first sorted out a very untidy plot. He used soil dug out from the plot as he went, and turned the weeds and grass into an excellent growing space in just a few weeks.

Weed-smothering

This is my favourite way of clearing a plot, and the method I used when I moved into my new house and began growing vegetables at the back of the garden. The area was a mixture of grass, weeds and bramble, so over a few weekends I pulled and dug out everything I could, including the larger and deep-rooted stuff, and then covered the soil with black weed-suppressant covering (see below), which removes sunlight and chokes the remaining weeds. This kept the plot weed-free over the winter, until I was ready to sow and plant. If your plot is in a particularly bad way, this process can take a whole season, but it will provide a great base for growing.

While you and your weed-suppressant are working hard to bring the plot back to life, try making the most of the available space by growing in containers. You can keep the containers on top of the covering you've laid down, and fill them with a mixture of multipurpose compost and some of the soil you've dug over. Remember that container veg will need more water than veg grown in the ground, but salad leaves, peas, chard and tomatoes all do well in containers.

Removing the weed-suppressant a few months later will reveal soil that's a doddle to dig over, which is great for anyone who is new to allotments or finds digging hard work. (That's all of us, by the way!) Earthworms will feast on the dying weeds too, leaving you very little to do. However, if you do have the urge to dig, you can always peel back the covering at your leisure and turn some of the soil. Popping the cover back over the soil will keep it clean until you're ready to sow and plant.

What is a weed-suppressant covering?

A weed-suppressant membrane is an industrial fabric that is laid over soil to suppress the growth of old weeds and stop new weeds from establishing. A quick search online will bring up a number of specific weed-suppressant products, at all manner of prices, but any old piece of tarpaulin, carpet or similar will also work perfectly well. Keep an eye out for skips, as these items can be readily found for free. On my garden patch I used a mixture of a surplus pond layer and old carpets left outside a local shop. You can also use cardboard, which boasts the added bonus of rotting down into the soil and improving the structure. In fact, some people use a sandwich method, placing cardboard in between the soil and a tarpaulin. Check out the local tip for large boxes in the cardboard recycling bins and ask in bike shops, too, as their bikes are often delivered to them in massive cardboard boxes.

Whatever you use, remember to fix your cover down firmly. The last thing you want is your neat and tidy membrane finding itself halfway across the allotment site after a particularly stiff gust of wind. Bricks or tent pegs will keep everything where it should be.

Improving the Soil

Yes! You've finally found the soil! It was there all along, underneath that jungle! The time has now come to get to know this wonderful resource intimately, for it is the most important element of your plot. Soil is living, breathing history, a result of thousands upon thousands of years of earth movements and weathering. I'm far from a geologist, but I do know that this vital growing base needs love, attention and management. Soil is a wild, natural product that was here long before us, and will be here long after us, too.

Forgive me a misty-eyed moment, but the first thing I did when I took on my plot was stand back and admire the soil, and visualize what this soil had seen – the different plot holders over the years, their motives for cultivating and their lives. Who put the old shed up? What had they grown? Where were they now? It was quite a feeling to imagine all the people who had spent time cultivating and tending to this soil in blissful summers and unforgiving winters, before passing the baton on to the next person. That next person was now me, and with this came a responsibility to be part of keeping this great tradition alive.

So soil is important in a historic context, but it's also what we grow our fruit and veg in. Being a raw material, soil needs a helping hand to get to a standard fit for cultivating, which is where we come in. Soil can be daunting to a beginner but it need not be as, essentially, requirements are simple. It needs nutrients, biodiversity and structure to flourish as a growing medium and, fortunately for us, a few simple steps can make it perfect for cultivation.

The first step is to get up close and personal with your soil to work out its make-up, as that will affect the measures you take to improve its condition. Of course, if you're lucky like I was first time around, you'll inherit lovely, rich, crumbly soil that has always been well nurtured and never neglected, and all you'll need to do is keep it topped up with nutrients. However, if you're bringing a plot back from the brink, you'll need to identify the soil's characteristics to determine the correct plan of action.

There are three main things to look out for: heaviness, drainage and whether the soil is acidic or chalky. A good place to start is by digging a small hole, about 50 cm (20 in) deep. This will help work out the structure of the soil. Is the soil crumbly on top, but heavier (and in some cases chunky and solid) further down? If so, this will mean that the soil may drain slowly. Conversely, the soil may be gravelly, which means fast-draining. An easy way to find this out is to pour some water into the hole and observe how quickly it drains away. If the drainage takes a long time (hours, in extreme cases) then you may experience problems with waterlogging that could hamper growth and even cause plants to rot. The stickiness of the wet soil will also help indicate what type you have. If you roll a handful into a ball and it keeps its shape, then you are likely to have heavy clay soil, but if it falls apart easily then the soil is light.

If your soil is heavy, the typical problems you will face include slow drainage and occasional waterlogging. The soil will be tough to work (especially when wet) and it will be slower to warm up in the spring than lighter soil, delaying the date that you can sow your seeds. Heavy soil will also be very hard when dry in the summer, making the surface solid. This causes a number of problems, such as water run-off and seeds struggling to break through after sowing. The soil is easily compacted if you walk on it, so try using a board when you do need to step on to the beds. However, there are some advantages to heavy or clay soil: it is usually fairly rich in nutrients and, once cultivated, is rich and fertile, so if you do discover clay, don't despair.

The good news for an allotmenteer with light soil is that it is much easier to work, which will certainly help your back. It warms quickly, too, so you can sow earlier than you would in heavier soil, and, being a faster-draining soil type, you are unlikely to have any problems with waterlogging. Light soil doesn't hold as many nutrients, however, so will require more work to increase fertility.

Digging

Unless you're in the enviable position of being handed a beautifully maintained plot and gorgeous, crumbly soil that just requires a light forking, you are likely to have to dig. Digging is a necessary evil for us vegetable growers, and there's no getting around it – digging is a slog. It is good exercise, though, and each section you complete presents a real feeling of fulfilment and satisfaction.

Timing is important, particularly where the type of soil is concerned. I rough dig my local clay soil in autumn (left any later and the rain makes it heavy and tough to work). Clay soil is also easily compacted when wet, especially when I clamber over the beds in my size 9s. Decent frosts help break up clay soils, so the longer you can leave your soil exposed to the winter elements the better. Once winter passes, I then work my soil to a finer tilth ready for sowing, using a fork and hoe or a little petrol tiller if I'm feeling lazy and have fallen behind (which is most years now). Light soils are more delicate and easier to work, but also susceptible to damage from poor weather. The best tactic here is to cover the soil in a thick layer of organic matter, ready to be dug in properly in spring.

There are several methods of digging, ranging from big effort 'double digging', through to no actual digging at all, a favourite of plot holders' backs everywhere.

Single Digging

Single digging is perhaps the most common digging method, and it basically means digging to the depth of a spade. Generally speaking, the single-dig method is sufficient to turn the soil and loosen weeds enough to whip them out without much hassle. The easiest way to single dig is to force the spade in with your foot, push the handle down and lift the soil, before tipping it back to whence it came. The soil will then be nicely loosened, especially if you tip it back in upside down. If your soil is full of weeds or grass, you can get hold of each clump and shake the soil out, returning most of the soil and goodness back to the ground and leaving you with just the weeds.

Double Digging

If the ground has never previously been cultivated, needs drainage improvement or you're particularly energetic and love some Krypton Factor-style logic, then double digging could be for you. It is proper graft, and involves digging trenches the depth of two spade blades, filling the bottom with organic matter and filling in again. Single digging will normally suffice, and double digging is only really necessary if your soil is very bad or you are starting pretty much from scratch.

No Digging

You may decide after all this that digging is, in fact, too much like hard work. Which is fine, as you could just forget about it and, well, not dig. This involves covering your soil with lots and lots of organic matter – a minimum of 5 cm (2 in) – and then letting the worms and insects work it in for you. The downside is that this relies on your soil being passable already, and if it's not, you'll need to do some serious double digging to get things underway. The process also takes a prolonged period of time, and is best done in autumn to give you a good chance of having something decent to show for the worms' efforts by the following spring.

Making Digging Life Easier

Like plot clearance, adopting a little-and-often approach is a winner when digging. Digging little and often is good for both body and mind. A morning's digging will bring plenty of aches and pains, especially if you're not used to doing it, so it is worth breaking up sessions if possible to ease the impact on the muscles. Learn to love a bath, too. Making time for a long, relaxing soak in the tub on digging days will help ease aches and pains in the following morning, especially with a nice glug of Radox.

When finances allow, get as good and lightweight a spade as possible. Spades found in the corner of an inherited shed are lovely and thrifty, but they're also often very old, heavy and cumbersome. A nice, light spade will be much easier to turn and far better for the achy muscles. Don't just dodge the wet days, either. I remember doing a summer digging session on a Saturday that just happened to be the hottest day of the year. It was hard work, and the heat made things twice as difficult. Digging when the ground is dry is tough going, as getting the spade into the soil requires much more effort. You need an overcast day that isn't too hot or too wet or too cold for good digging days. Clear as mud! Watch out for the earthworms. They're integral to the condition of the soil and do lots of hard work down there. I like to see plenty of earthworms, as it's a sign of good soil. At the same time, I'm not murderous or anything, but I do also like to help out the local blackbird when digging. He can spot a vulnerable worm a mile off …

The best digging tip I've received is to pull any weeds out as you go. This is another tip that sounds obvious in principle, but I've often thought, 'Oh, I'll pick them up later,' only to now realize that life is much easier if I do this while I go along. I miss half of them otherwise, either treading them back into the soil or too lazy after a hard morning's digging to actually pick them up.

And remember, digging is a marathon, not a sprint. I can often be found slumped over my spade, recharging the batteries before I get stuck into another row. Have a rest from time to time!

Adding Organic Matter

Feeding the soil to create a rich base for our plants is arguably the most important thing a veg grower does all year. The organic matter helps replenish the nutrients that have been taken out of the soil by the previous season's crops. Veg plants feed incredibly hard during the growing season, so replacing the lost goodness is vital for continuing success.

This needs to be done annually, and is traditionally done during the autumn, especially if you have heavy soil and plan to dig the organic matter in. The soil will still be dry and easier to work, and cold weather and frosts will later help to break up large clumps. While both heavy and light soils require replenishment, good-quality organic matter will also greatly help to add form and body to lighter soils. If you've got light soil, spread the organic matter over the surface to protect it from the winter elements, and dig in during early spring.

Often the organic matter you choose to add to your soil will depend on your own individual factors, such as space, cost and what is available locally. Here are several common types used on everyday allotment plots.

Animal Manure

Horse and cow manure is a traditional and popular organic matter among generations of gardeners. The very best muck is the jet black, well-rotted stuff that has been left for a year, and is often delivered to allotment plots on the back of trucks. Manure is also commonly available bagged up on the side of the road near local livery yards, ready to take away for a couple of quid. This is useful if you haven't got the space to take delivery of a truckload all at one time.

Animal manure is high in nutrients, making it ideal for digging into soil. A good load can cost up to £20, but this often depends on how keen people are to shift it. My local livery yard can't move it quick enough, and are more than happy for people to fill up trailers and bags from their muck mountain for nowt.

Seaweed

As someone in regular search of cheap alternatives to allotment equipment and resources, living near a river has been a rich source of freebies for me. Not only have I kept slugs away with broken shells, I've made a flotsam bench and plundered timber for a raised bed. Maybe most satisfying of all, I've manured several of my beds for the past few years using the bladderwrack seaweed that is washed up after every tide. If you've got access to the sea, a barrow full of the slimy, black weed can be gathered in no time at all.

Seaweed contains all the nutrients plants require for good growth, and can be dug straight in without washing the salt off. If you are collecting seaweed, take care not to remove too much from one area or to dislodge rocks in the process, as these provide an important habitat for estuary creatures such as crabs. A good pair of stout, grippy shoes is also advisable!

Leaf Mould

Leaf mould is low in nutrients, but is an excellent soil conditioner that helps maintain moisture, so is a good option for adding to light soils. I use leaf mould primarily to bulk up garden compost, although I find it an ace form of mulch on its own.

The mould is easy to make, but the leaves can take a year or so to rot down. Simply gather up the leaves, put them in a plastic bin liner and pierce a few holes into the bag. Hide the bag out of sight and forget about it for a year.

Garden Compost

Well-rotted, homemade compost is like black gold. High in nutrients, it is easy to make from an equal mixture of nitrogen-rich 'greens' (e.g. grass cuttings, vegetable peelings, spent veg plants) and carbon-rich 'browns' (e.g. cardboard, paper, straw), either in a designated compost bin, or piled up and covered with old carpet or tarpaulin. For me, this is by far the best manure and has certainly improved my harvests of nutrient-hungry crops, such as runner beans.

I've learned a few things along the way about what makes my compost bins tick. The size of the material you're adding to your bin is important, for one. Some ingredients, such as eggshells and woodier cuttings, can take a lot longer to break down than normal wet additions like veg peelings and old veg plants. I've found breaking up the eggshells and chopping the cuttings into smaller pieces can help speed up the composting process.

A good mix of ingredients is key. Essentially, you need equal amounts of green material, your kitchen scraps (veg peelings, etc.) and 'browns'. For browns, I often use cardboard – the bog-standard parcel-type stuff is best. You need to regularly check the contents of your compost bin to make sure that your compost isn't getting too soggy. If it looks as if it might be, that's the time to add more cardboard. Make sure you rip it up into small chunks, though.

I've also found heat to be really important to the composting speeds. One of my 'dalek' compost bins is positioned in a sunny spot, and rots down much, much quicker than the one that spends a large part of the day in shade. Make sure the lids are on tight, as they help to keep the heat in (and also stop them blowing away in a strong wind).

The only other slight problem is that the contents of a dalek-style bin can be tricky to turn, but I tend to stick a fork in every so often which helps keep things on the move. One excellent tip I've picked up is to put the daleks next to each other. That way you can easily move the contents between bins, rather than turning the mix in the bins.

I was lucky to inherit two daleks from a neighbouring plot holder for free, but if you're not so fortunate, try your local council. Many sell them at a reasonable price, or check out www.getcomposting.com for a company that works with local authorities in the UK to provide residents with low-cost compost bins and accessories, wormeries and kitchen composters.

Compost heaps are a cheap alternative, and, as I have mentioned before, can be made by nailing three wooden pallets together on their sides in an open box shape, and filling the space up with compostable materials. Cover with an old carpet to insulate and keep the warmth in.

Final Soil Prep

Most vegetable plants can be grown from seed sown directly into the soil, normally in rows or clusters and at dates depending on local temperatures. To give the seeds the best chance of germination and strong growth, the soil needs to be prepared beforehand. The aim is to achieve as fine a crumbly surface as possible, free of anything that might harm the seed during this important time in its life cycle.

The easiest way to do this is to use a mini petrol tiller, but these are an expensive luxury for an allotment plot. They do produce beautiful soil, however, so if you can get hold of one for a few hours then your seeds will love you for it. Otherwise, a good old hoe will produce a nice tilth.

It just takes a bit more work, but after all the digging some simple hoeing will be a doddle.

To prepare an area for seed sowing, use the hoe to break up the first 5–10 cm (2–4 in) of soil and any other large chunks of soil, removing stones and weeds as you go. It's a short job if you prepare an area as you are ready to sow it, rather than trying to do all the beds in one go. Seeds are sown at different intervals, so it makes sense to take this approach, as nicely prepared soil might be trodden on or disrupted if the beds aren't needed at once, and the job would need to be done all over again later on. Try to avoid preparing soil after or during rain, as the soil can become sticky and difficult to work in the wet. The surface can also dry to a hard crust if the soil becomes really wet.

Finish off by raking the surface level by working the rake up and down the bed, removing any extra stones or weeds that appear. Keep raking until the surface is light and well loosened – now it's ready for some seeds.

CHAPTER 6

Sowing Seeds

As with most allotment tasks, sowing seeds is all about timing. Different seeds require different soil temperatures for germination, so determining if the time is right for sowing is vital for successful germination. Spring is one of the busiest times on the plot, as pretty much all the grower's seeds will be sown during this time. As the weather warms the soil up – hey presto! – the exhilaration and anticipation of the new growing season is upon us again.

Location plays an important factor in this equation, as I'm gently reminded on Twitter every now and again. I'll publish a smiley, happy blog post well before the clocks have changed, extolling the virtues of seeds you can sow in February when my Twitter friends in the north of England will point out that my little south-east pocket is practically balmy compared to other areas of the country. Snow? What snow?

As silly as it sounds, don't forget to read the seed packets. They will tell you the correct temperatures required for germination, as well as provide an idea of when the seeds can typically be sown, so you can work out what to sow when. A soil thermometer is a worthwhile investment if you're looking for accurate readings, either inside or outside a greenhouse. Getting an idea of temperatures during the different times of the day will help you determine whether the time is right for sowing.

Seed packets will offer other useful advice, such as whether seedlings need some shade or full sun, or whether you need to avoid sowing or planting out until after the last frosts have passed. This is particularly relevant to tender plants such as tomatoes, runner beans and courgettes, all of which are very susceptible to frost, so it is vital to avoid subjecting them to cold nights. Should you be unsure of when your last frost might be, a quick search online will soon tell you.

Although no one cares much for weeds, they are a useful indicator of whether the soil is warm enough to sow your seeds successfully. When weeds start coming through, it means the temperature is sufficient for plant life to survive, so seeds that are sown then should germinate and grow on.

Unused seeds will last more than one season, but need to be stored in a cool, dark place to maintain their dormant state. I keep mine in a tin under the stairs. Check over your old seeds in between the seasons to make sure they're all still in date. Some seeds lose viability quicker than others (parsnips, for example), but just because they are out of date doesn't mean they won't necessarily germinate. Chances are, however, that germination rates will be reduced the more out of date the seeds are.

One thing I've definitely learned over the years is not to rush into sowing. From my experience, if you think you're running behind, your timing is actually just about right – a little bit late is better than a little bit cold. Waiting until mid-April or even early May to sow is really no great shakes in the grand scheme of things, and seedlings will grow quickly in the higher temperatures and longer days of these two months. Of course, we're all prone to excitable temptation and early sowing, but should any seeds make their way into the ground before time, these need to be seen as bonus crops – you can cross your fingers for an early harvest, but don't rely on them.

Warming Up the Soil

I know, I get it. You're getting impatient. You've dug and dug in preparation for this moment. You're sure those nights are drawing out. You want to sow. There must be a way of warming this soil up! Well, there are one or two tricks that are used to increase soil temperature and allow for earlier sowing, and none of these are particularly expensive if you're prepared to do some rummaging, reusing and recycling.

Coldframes are popular among gardeners who do not have the luxury of a greenhouse. An effective coldframe can boost temperatures by several degrees, meaning seeds can be sown earlier than if they were out in the open. They are readily available to buy, but can cost anything from £30 to hundreds of pounds. However, they're also a doddle to make if you're happy with a more rudimentary alternative. The easiest and cheapest way to knock up a coldframe is to arrange some bricks in a rectangle (around four high) on the soil that will receive your seeds, with a sheet of glass on

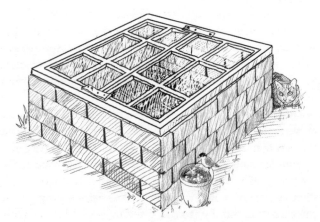

top. Old windows are a good choice, and can be found in skips or at the local tip.

Cloches work in the same way as coldframes, and traditionally were made of glass. Sophisticated versions can look beautiful in a garden, but are often expensive. My favourite cheap and cheerful, alternative way of making a functional cloche is to cut a large plastic bottle in half and place the halves over the spot where you're planning to plant a seed or seedling. When I first took on my allotment, we used this method to grow and protect early squash and tomato plants.

And if the good old weed-suppressing, soil-protecting, tool-covering tarpaulin doesn't have enough uses, you can also repurpose it once more for some late winter, early spring soil-warming. Spread a black tarpaulin over your beds and this will heat the soil quicker as the days get longer and warmer. This is an excellent approach for early root crops such as parsnips, early carrots and radishes.

Pot or Direct Sowing?

Many gardeners choose to start some seeds off in small pots and plant out later, rather than sowing everything directly into the ground. There is no right or wrong answer when deciding which method to use, but starting seedlings off in pots does give a number of advantages over direct sowing.

Pot sowings can be started off in a greenhouse, coldframe or even on a sunny windowsill and grown until the weather is warm enough for them to be transplanted outside into an open plot. This brings the growing season forward a few weeks, as the seedlings can grow on in relative warmth while you wait for the milder temperatures the plants ultimately require. Pots are portable, too, which means you can put your seedlings out in the sun during the day, and bring them back in when the temperature dips at night. This allows the plants to acclimatize to their new environment before they are planted out, strengthening the plant and reducing the risk of loss.

Germination can also be improved with a good-quality multipurpose compost. This can be bought from any nursery or garden centre and will be specially treated so that it is free of disease and weed seeds. Multipurpose compost is traditionally a blend of peat and other materials, such as bark or green compost, as well as fertilizer and lime. The idea is to create a pH (acid) and nutrient level that is suitable for growing a wide range of plants. The compost will be fine and enriched with nutrients, too, providing a better and more reliable base for germination than the soil in allotment beds.

Multipurpose compost can be expensive, but you do get what you pay for. A decent one is vital to a successful sowing season, so buy the best you can. Ideally, the texture of compost should be fairly fine, as this will help hold moisture and allow seedlings the chance to break through. Sometimes, cheaper, own-brand composts from larger stores contain lots of bark and this can be a problem for finer seeds such as carrots and leeks. If you're worried, try sieving the compost with a garden sieve first to get the soil nice and fine.

If you're on a budget or enjoy owning the whole process from start to finish, making your own is easy, and can be done by mixing equal parts of leaf mould, kitchen compost and soil (molehills are good for this), before passing it through a garden sieve. Homemade sowing compost won't be sterilized, so expect some weeds to come through and compete with your seedlings, but these can be pulled out easily enough. Making up your own soil is a lovely thing to do, and not just as a money-saver. Mixing the ingredients is very satisfying and the result feels wonderful when running it through your fingers. Expect funny looks when bagging up molehills, though … To help make your compost go further, try sowing more than one seed in a pot. For example, I sow five or six pea seeds in 13 cm (5 in) pots and break them up when planting out. I've done the same with broad beans, French beans, runners and mangetout, which all have grown on perfectly well. The same size pot can also accommodate two to three tomato, squash and courgette seeds.

Like container plants, pots dry out quickly, too, especially if you are using cheaper compost. Make sure you check for dryness regularly, and water whenever the soil is looking parched. Fill the pots with soil to within a couple of centimetres of the top, and this will catch the water, so that it stays in the pot rather than running off. Use a watering can with a fine rose to water, so that the soil isn't sloshed away and the seeds dislodged, and don't forget to label the pot with the seed type and day it was sown. I am useless at this, and regularly pay the price when trying to remember which was a good variety, or whether a batch of seeds should have germinated yet!

Direct Sowing

Although pot sowing has its advantages, there are still reasons to direct sow as well. The main benefit is to plants that don't like root disturbance, such as parsnips and carrots. Sowing them in one place and leaving them be will ensure good growth much more than moving them around. Direct sowing also makes sowing lots of seeds a quick and easy job. Again, carrots and parsnips are good examples here, as seeds are small and dainty, so sowing thickly will increase germination chances. Of course, it is also much cheaper to sow direct, as there is no need for bags of multipurpose compost, pots, coldframes or greenhouses.

For the best direct-sowing results, prepare the soil to a fine tilth, and use a hoe to separate the soil into a shallow groove. If sowing in straight lines, use two sticks as a guide, tied together with some string and popped into the ground at each end of the row. Water along the

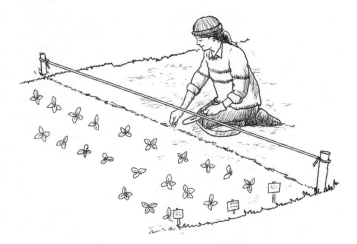

bottom of the groove before sowing, and sow seeds as per packet instructions. Try to get them spread evenly so that seedlings aren't patchy along the row. Sowing a cluster of seeds at the end of each row provides useful backup for filling in any gaps that do arise from patchy germination. This is particularly handy for plants that don't mind being transplanted, such as peas, beetroot and French beans, but it is worth trying for any direct sowing.

Cover the seeds with the soil you moved when creating the groove, unless your soil is heavy or clay-based, in which case the surface is likely to crisp up as the heat from the sun increases and produce a rock-hard barrier that seeds can struggle to penetrate. If this is likely, fill the groove with multipurpose compost. I was given this tip as a way of preventing the soil crusting over and making life difficult for germinating carrots, as not many of my seedlings were strong enough to push through my heavy soil. By sowing the seeds as normal, but covering them in multipurpose compost, the top is soft and light, giving the seedlings a good chance of showing their face.

Again, water using the rose fitting on the watering can, and then date and mark where and what you sowed. As well as reminding you of what was sown, this helps make sure you don't trample all over everything later in a fit of forgetfulness! Familiarize yourself with what the seedling looks like so that you can spot it coming up among any weeds. Some of the more expensive seed packets carry images of the seedlings on the back, but if not you'll find a picture online.

Maximizing Germination

Sowing seeds can be a source of great joy – or of equally great frustration. The sight of those tiny plants pushing their way up through the soil is a wonderful moment, but the forlorn daily checking of stubborn seeds that are refusing to play ball can drive you mad. Generally, most seeds are fairly uncomplicated but there are a few things you can do to help as many germinate as possible. Reliable germination is a key factor in growing food, especially if you're aiming to save money or become more self-sufficient. Sowing at the right time according to your local conditions, having good-quality soil and following the seed packet instructions (men, we don't read instructions …) will all contribute, but it is also important not to forget about the seeds once they're in the soil, as they'll still need your attention just as much.

Seeds appreciate consistency and need the right amounts of water, light and heat – this may sound obvious, but it is very easy to get carried away and try to germinate a melon outside on a patio in March just because the BBC's Carol said the week was going to be unseasonably warm (I know, I've done this). Seeds won't necessarily need watering every day (too much water can cause waterlogging and rot them), but try to get into a regular pattern so that the soil doesn't dry out. Don't forget to keep your seeds snug either. Make sure they're sown in a sunny spot, and if they're in pots you can even move them around to get the best of the sunshine. Most seeds need temperatures of 18°C (65°F) or more to germinate, and the weather can be very unpredictable during the main spring sowing period. If cold weather is forecast, cover your pots with horticultural fleece or bubble wrap to help bring the temperature up a notch.

Don't be afraid to keep sowing if nothing happens in the time that you expected it to. There are far more seeds in a seed packet than most of us will ever use, so don't be shy – just chuck them in the ground! If nothing at all happens with a row or pots of seeds, consider buying a fresh packet. The seeds could be a bad packet or have lost viability. To check the condition of old seeds, try doing a germination test. This is a quick and easy procedure and well worth doing before you go spending money on new seeds. Place a sheet of damp kitchen roll on a plate, and sprinkle ten or so seeds onto the paper. Cover it with cling film, note the date and store in a warm place. Check for germination after a few days and then a week. If seven or eight seeds germinate, you know you have a 75 per cent chance of germination from that packet. Any less, and it's time to treat yourself to some fresh ones.

'OMG, I've got seedlings!'

Spring is here, the sun is warming and it's still light outside when you return home. There's a tingle in your tummy – butterflies of excitement. A wonderful feeling of expectation takes over every time you visit the allotment or go out into the garden. This, my friends, is the exhilarating anticipation that comes with waiting for those first seedlings to gently force themselves up through the soil.

I first experienced this feeling when I got a greenhouse in my garden at home. It meant I could check on my seedlings numerous times a day: when I got up, when I returned from work and before I went to bed. Every time I marched down the garden the same sense of excitement came over me. Would there be any germination today? How many seeds? How much more had the little seedlings grown?

This feeling is one of the best of the year: the start of a new cycle, the strange, ambitious idea that these tiny infant plants will grow on and provide food by the time the summer finishes. You immediately develop a feeling of responsibility for them when they do arrive. You suddenly want to nurture them and give them the best possible chance of growing into full-blown plants. Spring is the main sowing time and a critical period for us allotmenteers and our precious plants, so giving them the best possible start in life is vital.

Like seeds, baby plants also like consistency. I try to get into a watering routine fitted around my everyday life. I like to water seedlings every day at the same time, and normally do this just after dinner. With the sun going down, there is less chance of the water being quickly sucked up by the heat as it might on a sunny morning. The flipside of evening watering is that damp surfaces can bring the local slug and snail populations out, and these are the biggest single threat to seedlings the length and breadth of the country. (More on those little critters on page 139.)

You'll still need to use a watering can with a rose head, so that the plants get a nice sprinkle. If your seedlings are in pots, you can leave them in saucers of water. The water will be absorbed gently through the holes in the bottom of the pots, ensuring the seedlings get exactly the amount of water they desire.

Steady temperatures are also helpful, but are often out of our hands. Spring can prove tricky as the nights are often cold but the days can be very warm, particularly if your seedlings are in the greenhouse. Generally, plants that are outdoors can cope okay with temperature fluctuations, but decent sunshine will rocket warmth in the greenhouse and stress the plants, so do all you can to get some cool in there by opening doors and windows. In a worse-case scenario, plants can literally be frazzled by the heat, as happened to some very healthy rosemary plants after I neglected to open the door one morning. Some greenhouses have automatic vents, and you can also buy special paint that helps shade the plants from too much heat.

As always, keep an eye on the weather forecast in case of frosty nights. Young seedlings can be killed off by sharp frosts unless they're protected overnight by fleece or bubblewrap. Don't let seedlings overcrowd each other, either in pots or rows. Too many seedlings will mean too much competition for nutrients and water, so make sure there is enough to go around by pulling out the seedlings you don't need. If you have room, try replanting some of the seedlings for bonus crops. This can be useful if germination has been patchy in a row.

Hardening Off and Planting Out

Any early-season seedlings raised in a greenhouse or indoors will need to be 'hardened off' before they can be planted out into an open allotment or vegetable bed. This is merely a process of acclimatization for young plants that have become accustomed to the cosiness of undercover living, before you fling them out to face the elements. A greenhouse environment is much warmer and more humid than outside, with little or no air circulation, so moving plants outside permanently without acclimatization can cause damage. Instead, this needs to be done gradually over a week or two so that by the time the plant is ready to go into its final spot, it is strong enough to cope with all that the weather can throw at it.

A fortnight of progressive hardening off will give plants plenty of time to adapt, ready for planting out. For the first week, bring the plants out of the greenhouse first thing in the morning and then place them back inside for the night. During the second week, begin to leave the plants outside permanently but cover with fleece or bubblewrap if the temperature is predicted to drop. Towards the end of the week, ditch the fleece and prepare to plant out. Some hardier plants, such as peas, leeks and brassicas, will let you get away with shorter hardening off periods, but stick to the fortnight timescale for more delicate plants such as tomatoes, squashes and courgettes.

If like me you're prone to bouts of disorganization and forgetfulness, stick a prominent note up on the fridge or similar to remind you to put the plants away. Some trays to hold the plants are a real winner, too. During peak sowing and growing times there will be all manner of plants hardening off, and picking up a few trays to move outside quickly and efficiently is far less of a pain than fifty-odd individual pots every morning and night – particularly if you have indeed forgotten about your plants and you're clambering around in the dark in pyjamas trying to put them back into the greenhouse!

Watch out for plants bought from nurseries and garden centres, as there is no way of telling how well these plants have been hardened off (if at all), so make sure you do some hardening off with them before planting out. They may have been hardened off perfectly well, but it is better to be safe than sorry if you're parting with your hard-earned cash.

Once happily hardened, plants grown in pots will need planting out into your veg beds to mature. Again, this is an easy job but does require some organization and a bit of good old common sense. For example, choosing the appropriate weather for planting out is important. Make sure there are no frosts forecast, or that you're not planting out on a windy day. Plants need a few days to establish so it pays not to stick them straight out into a barracking from the elements. It sounds daft, but the weather forecast is a gardener's friend, so don't forget to check it before deciding to plant out. Some plants are hardier than others and will take some grief, but others can be delicate. The broad beans I subjected to a dumping of snow sulked for a few days but perked up eventually, while a single frost can finish off even the strongest of tomato plants. You can't beat a good drop of rain to help a plant overcome relocation, so planting out before a shower is perfect if you can manage to find such a slot!

Water your plants prior to taking them out of their pots as this will help keep the soil compacted around the roots – the more soil that stays around there, the better. Removing the plant safely takes some practice, but I've found the best way to get the plant out of its pot is to hold the pot in one hand, turn it upside down and tap the bottom a few times. This should loosen the whole thing and a gentle shake will release the plant into your free hand. Once out of the pot, I find handling the plant around the root ball, or where the most soil is holding on, is the safest place. Don't pick up by the stem, as this is the weakest spot.

Prepare planting holes before removing plants from pots so that the time out of soil is limited, making sure each plant will have enough room (seed packets will give you these measurements). Discard any errant weeds and anything else that might hinder growth, such as large stones. Add some goodness to the bottom of the hole, such as manure or kitchen compost. A trowel-full will suffice, as overdoing it can make the soil too hot or rich and damage roots rather than help feed them. Fill the hole with water and wait for it to drain away – you might need to give the soil a few prods with your hoe to speed this up. Pop the plant into the hole, and gently press it down into the soil, and then fill the hole around the plant with the soil that has been dug out. The plant will need pressing down again to make sure that it can't budge in the hole, so keep doing this as you fill. For depth, a good rule of thumb is to plant the seedling at about the depth it was in the container.

One of the best tips I have picked up came from my mum during one of our regular Saturday afternoon plot sessions. She taught me to plant in recesses, so that water stayed in and around the base of the plant when watered, rather than running off. To achieve a recess, push the plant deeper into the soil and/or build a mound around the plant so that the water is caught and can't escape – like creating a little moat. I initially started using this super planting method for squash plants, but now I use it for pretty much everything that I plant out. The beauty of recess planting is that the water stays around the base of the plant where it is needed for multiple days, both reducing the amount of time I have to spend lugging a watering can about and ensuring the plant is getting the right levels of water when it wants. Even in my greenhouse, the recess has remained moist for three days during hot, high summer.

Don't forget, your seedlings need you after they've been planted out! Keep an eye on them, especially in dry weather, as they'll need regular watering to ensure the roots grow strong even if you do use the recess planting

tip. If your site is exposed, consider staking the plants to support them in windy weather. This is easily done by poking a cane into the ground next to the plant, and tying the stem to the cane with gardening string.

More on Watering

The problem with watering is that it can be a bit boring, especially if the water tap is a couple of plots away. I love sowing, planting and nurturing, and I don't even mind a spot of weeding, but watering is a chore. Discipline, therefore, is very much required, because watering is vital for a plant at many stages of its life cycle. Seeds need water (and warmth) to provide the strength to break the seed shell and start germination, and the seedlings need plenty of watering as they only have a small root growth, so can't reach right down to the moisture retained in the soil. When plants begin to flower they will also need regular and consistent watering, particularly where beans and peas are concerned. This is when the plants form pods, and require water to provide a productive harvest.

Once plants are established, many of the common varieties of veg grown on an allotment, such as leeks, radishes, carrots, beetroot, purple sprouting broccoli, sprouts, onions, spring greens, parsnips and herbs, are actually quite content in dry conditions, meaning you can lay off them and reduce watering to once a week. Other plants will still require more care with watering, especially short-rooted, leafy veg like salads and peas, as well as anything in a container as the soil will dry out very quickly. Leafy crops are thirsty drinkers – watch out for wilting, but don't panic if the leaves do wilt as a good soaking will soon perk up the plants. Tomatoes, strawberries, squashes, courgettes and cucumbers are mostly made up of water

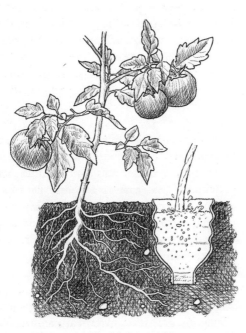

so will need more liquid if you want to grow good-sized specimens.

With all this in mind, putting together a watering routine is a good idea, especially in dry weather. I live in one of the driest counties in the UK, so I have to keep at the watering if I want a productive harvest. As a rule of thumb, I try to water my established veg once a week, my squash, courgette, tomatoes and greenhouse plants three times a week, with daily checks on any little seedlings and container plants if I can. Concentrating on the plants that need the most water reduces the amount of time I need to spend watering, and allows me to use the time I'm at the plot more wisely.

If getting down to your allotment to do the watering is tricky for you, there are ways in which you can further reduce the time spent watering. DIY self-watering systems can be made by cutting plastic bottles in half and pushing the top half neck first into the soil next to your bigger plants, such as tomatoes and squashes. Punch a few holes in the bottle lid and push the bottle down so that the cut edge is level with the soil, and then the water will gather in the vessel and slowly trickle through the neck to the plant, drawing out the time that the water is feeding the plant. Potted seedlings and plants can be left on trays filled with water so that the roots can pull required water up through the bottom of the pot, again increasing the time that a plant feeds. Mulching plants around the base with straw or compost helps keep moisture in, while watering in the early morning and late evening reduces evaporation as the temperatures and sunlight are lower. Plant out in recesses and use a hoe to loosen the soil around plants, as this stops the water running off when the ground is like concrete.

A decent downpour will cheer everything up and get water where the plants need it, but don't overestimate the power of showers or light rain during summer. Soil can become rock-solid in the warmer months, which will often mean quick showers have no real effect on plants. You might need to water even though there has been some rain. A proper downpour is what you really want, and as a GYOer you will learn to love the rain when no one else does. Rain is miserable and ruins picnics, beer garden pints and camping trips and generally keeps us all inside, but don't let it get you down. Next time a summer barbecue is washed out by an afternoon's rain, just think how much the veggies are enjoying it. As my mum always says, you can't beat a lovely drop of rain.

CHAPTER 7

Pests and Diseases

A good friend of mine bought me a very entertaining little book as a birthday present a couple of years back. It's called *50 Ways to Kill a Slug*, and contains all manner of serious and silly ways in which gardeners can outwit their number one enemy. (For the record, I enjoy the bloodbath of mowing the lawn just after some rain ...) I very much liked the nice illustrations and the idea that there were so many tips, tricks and old gardeners' tales for dealing with slimies, but it also served to bring me to a comforting and almost Buddhist conclusion: veg-growing (particularly organically) sometimes means holding your hands up and admitting defeat to many of the pesky pests that inhabit the same environment as our beloved crops. To use a common phrase, you win some and you lose some.

I normally lose a crop a year to a pest or disease. At first I was cut deep by my failures, but nowadays I'm okay with this. Like death and taxes, that's life. If a snail can climb several metres up a tree to eat plums, like plenty did one year, I feel you've just got to sit back, be dignified in defeat and say 'fair play'. Over time, I've come to see the organic gardener versus local wildlife battle as a friendly one, like neighbouring cricket teams competing on the village green. I wouldn't say I like these vegetable garden adversaries, but I've built up a genuine respect for them and our annual skirmishes. In fact, if this were cricket, I'd sit around at the end of the season and have a beer with those bothersome pests.

For me, accepting that some crops will get munched or diseased is the best possible advice apart from the practical prevention tips. Don't let crop losses get you down, and learn to look on the bright side. You might lose your brassicas to the cabbage whites one year, but you might have beaten the blackfly and kept slug loss to a minimum. Revel in the victories, learn from the losses and adapt your growing for the next season.

With an acceptance that pests and diseases will always be there, you can then set about understanding how they function in their environment and begin to try and formulate plans for how you anticipate and respond to them. This is the key – taking action to try to reduce their chances, learning to spot the signs early, and then dealing efficiently with what you can to give your plants the best chance of survival.

Common Pests

Slugs and Snails

One of the biggest threats to a successful allotment year, slugs and snails are everywhere and if together in force they can munch through rows and rows of baby seedlings

and plants in a single night. Every year their voracity is bemoaned on my Twitter feed, in what seems like a losing battle. From my experience, night-time torchlight hunts are very effective at removing large amounts of slugs and snails, especially if there has been rain. I find that in the days after a good slug hunt in damp conditions, the population reduces significantly. You'll need to either humanely despatch them or find somewhere a long way from your plot to release them, though scientists found recently that snails placed or tossed within 65 metres (213 feet) of your plot will use a homing instinct to find their way back!

Sprinkling spiky things around the base of your plants helps keep some slugs and snails at bay as they don't like crawling across rough surfaces. Broken eggshells or seashells or grit are commonly used for this purpose, while strips of copper provide a mild electric shock when crawled over. Smaller seedlings can be covered overnight by protective cloches, or plastic bottles cut in half.

Looking at the bigger picture and keeping the allotment tidy can also help considerably. Scruffy, overgrown spots in the garden are very welcoming habitats for slugs and snails, so remove any unwanted bushes or plants as soon as you can as they can harbour literally hundreds of slimy things. Unused piles of boxes, pots, timber or logs can also provide a home for a slug or snail, so get rid of anything that contains a nook or cranny and this will greatly reduce the number of opportunities for them to live on your plot.

Cabbage White Caterpillars

Back in the summer of 2013, I learned a valuable lesson: always listen to your wife. When she tells you that something needs doing promptly, she is always right. Had I listened to my wife, the brassica massacre of 2013 could have been avoided.

Cabbage white caterpillars love brassicas. The butterflies lay their eggs on the plants during high summer, and once hatched, the familiar black and yellow caterpillars set about the leaves of brassica plants at a speed which it is impossible to match. Before you know it, a whole crop is wiped out, and with brassicas generally being much needed winter-cropping plants, this is a veritable allotment disaster. In 2013, I suffered my first total crop loss, courtesy of these caterpillars. I'd become complacent as the plants I'd grown at my allotment were always untouched by them, but when I switched to growing veg in my garden, everything changed. Cabbage whites were everywhere, and my wife quickly spotted this, urging me time and time again to protect the plants by putting some netting over the top. 'It'll be fine', I'd say. 'There's plenty of time.' Except there wasn't, and by the time I'd snapped out of my lackadaisical mood, the caterpillars were hatched and it was too late.

I was down in the doldrums over this loss for some time, but, these things are sent to test us, and we're only as good as the lessons we learn from our mistakes. Primarily, I learned that cabbage white caterpillars are unstoppable once they get established, so the key is prevention. Netting is the only way in which I've successfully defended my brassicas from cabbage whites, and that's netting from the minute they are planted out. These days the netting goes straight over the plants, and stays on until November. The netting needs to be a fine mesh – as I've mentioned before, I've found that scaffolding net is excellent for the job and it can be had for free if you're lucky and find an amenable scaffolder with a spare roll or two at the end of a job, as I did. Build a frame with bamboo canes and string or cable ties, and attach the net with pegs. Make sure there are no holes for the butterflies to get in. If there are gaps, they will definitely find them. Weight the bottom down with bricks, and secure the netting with tent pegs.

And don't forget to make the structure big enough for the plants to grow into.

Inevitably, some butterflies might find a way into your fortress, so it is important regularly to check on the plants. If possible, morning and evening are preferable as soon as the butterflies are spotted. Look out for little, yellow eggs on the leaves. Remove them before they hatch and your plants will live to fight another day.

Blackfly

Commonly known as lovers of broad beans, blackflies unfortunately attack other allotment favourites, such as courgettes, French beans and runner beans. They're sap-sucking insects that attack young plants in large clusters, weakening the plant and stunting its growth. Like cabbage white caterpillars, blackfly can take hold of a plant swiftly, so regular checks are the best way of keeping the pests at bay. If you spot an infestation, spray them with hot, soapy water, and then carefully rub the flies off the plants. I can't describe how odd squishing blackfly between fingers feels, but it really is strange. You'll hopefully know what I mean, as I think this might be one of those things that only a veg grower understands. You have to stick at the checking, squirting and squishing, as getting rid of them may take a week or so, but I've found that eventually this method does work. I'm not sure Fairy Liquid is strictly organic, but it's good enough for me …

Blackfly can be quite debilitating to a plant, but don't panic if you discover them. It's not the end of your crops – just be frequent and consistent with the soapy spraying and squashing, and with a bit of luck, all will be okay.

A preventative tip worth considering is growing nasturtiums nearby as so-called 'sacrificial' plants. A box of young nasturtiums is as cheap as chips to buy and if

there is one thing that blackfly love more than broad beans, it's nasturtiums. The blackfly will attack the nasturtiums instead of the veg plant and although this method cannot be guaranteed as 100 per cent successful, I've found that it does reduce the amount of blackfly on the beans. What's more, they look pretty planted out among the beans and courgettes.

Whitefly

Whiteflies are other flies that suck on the sap of plants. These too have taken a chunk out of my brassica crop, but can be deterred by planting marigolds around your plot since the flies don't like the smell of the flowers. I use African marigolds for maximum smelliness and have found that the amount of whitefly was reduced considerably.

Birds

Watching a cheeky bird swoop down to nick a raspberry from your allotment can be a lovely sight, until you remember that's one less fruit going on your breakfast. They're agile and quick to strike, so if you find that the local birds are feasting on your plot goodies, the easiest way to stop this is netting. Those with the time and resources will build handsome cages, some so impressive in scale that you can walk in and tend to your plants. However, cheap netting propped up by bamboo canes and held in place with bricks will keep the birds off equally as well for a fraction of the cost and energy.

Woodpigeons are probably the most serious bird threat to veg plots. As well as fruit, they enjoy a brassica or two and will peck at leaves until there are nothing but stalks and empty leaves left. Watch out for them pinching newly planted onion and garlic bulbs out of the soil, too.

I save my old cans and plastic milk bottles to put over the tops of bamboo canes which I stick into the ground next to my plants. The cans and bottles rattle in the wind, acting as bird-scarers. Another plot holder recommended putting sticks in the ground, tying string between the tops of the sticks and then hanging CDs downwards on more strings. This method dangles the shiny discs just a few inches from the plants, again scaring the birds away. If you're like me and have a multitude of rubbish CDs from years gone by, this is a great way of clearing some space on the living room shelves.

As you get further into your allotment adventure, you will come across other pests including those local to your plots, such as deer, squirrels, badgers, moles and even cats. There is nothing worse than cats using your plot as a toilet, but you might be eating cake or something as you read this so I'll stop there. Chatting to your neighbouring plot holders is the best way of discovering these local pests and how to deal with them. Your fellow growers will be a fount of knowledge and picking their brains is one of the most useful ways of learning. Chat to them, and soak up everything they've got to say because pretty much all of it will be relevant.

Diseases

As with most pests, prevention is much easier and successful than reacting to problems as they happen, leaving you on the back foot and full of allotment anxiety. Disease is a master of stealth, and will set in quickly and quietly, often before a plot holder even notices. Unfortunately, once a disease sets in, it will grip your plants quickly and by the time symptoms show themselves, infection can be out of control, leaving a row of dying plants. Disease also spreads rapidly across the plot, so removing and destroying infected plants as quickly as possible is good practice, as soul-crushing as that may be. Ideally, the bonfire is the best place for diseased plants – don't be tempted to put them in your compost bins or dig them into the ground. That will only spread the disease further into your soil next year. Destroying infected plants will also win you favour with your allotment neighbours, as it will prevent transmission to their plots.

Ensuring all the right tasks are done to grow decent plants from seed will help equip them with the strength to give diseases a decent fight, so do your best to water and protect in the build-up to summer. Most diseases are environmental and are best controlled by maintaining a clean, tidy allotment with healthy soil and surroundings. Clear away dead and decaying plants as soon as you can, and work on improving drainage if your plot suffers from waterlogging. Good drainage will stop waterlogging and prevent rot, which decays plant tissue and can cause root diseases such as parsnip canker. If there is an area on your allotment that drains poorly, avoid planting anything until you have found a way to improve the water run-off.

Common diseases such as downy mildew, rusts and blight are caused by lack of airflow, humidity and moisture build-up around the plants. These diseases spread easily, so follow the planting guidelines on the seed packets and don't plant too close together. The consistency and quality of watering is very important for disease prevention, and too much watering can actually be detrimental, drowning roots or introducing excessive moisture content around the plants. Watering in the morning helps reduce build-up as the sun evaporates moisture. Powdery mildew is caused by prolonged periods of dry weather, and can be avoided by watering regularly during dry periods and mulching around the plant to keep moisture in around the base.

Growing disease-resistant or disease-tolerant cultivars is another way of reducing the chance of infections on your allotment plot. There are many of these types of seeds available in the shops, and although they can be expensive, their increased reliability can be worth the extra money if you find you're regularly experiencing the same problems with disease. Useful examples of these cultivars include the rust-resistant leek Oarsman F1, blight-tolerant tomato Fandango, canker-resistant parsnip Albion and blight-resistant potato Sarpo.

CHAPTER 8

Harvesting

Ah, harvesting time. The culmination of all our hard work, when the sun shines and we make hay. Harvesting any crop brings with it a heady feeling of triumph; a moment of genuine buzz, whether you're digging up potatoes, sucking up the heady scent of lifted leeks or reaching high for runner beans. I have been known to clench fists and whoop with excitement at the sight of certain vegetables and fruit reaching harvestable stage. And why shouldn't we bask in the glow of harvesting success, given that we've nurtured these plants for months and months? That's a labour of love right there, and the fruits of our labour are just desserts for the effort.

Harvesting can also be a time when we finally nail that nemesis vegetable, after years of trying. I can't deny a little jig of joy when I grew my first cauliflower, and as my wife will tell you, I hate dancing. But this was a beautiful, chunky cauli, notoriously tricky to grow, sitting proudly on my plot ready for picking and coating with lashings of cheese sauce. Celebration was deserved.

Effective and neat harvesting can also contribute greatly to the quality of the produce on your plate as well as the level of your morale. Timing, the speed in which crops make their way to the kitchen, weather and the tools you use (or don't use) can also play a big part, and while it can be tempting to just swipe produce off the plants and out the ground in a fit of excitement, I'd definitely recommend being measured and prepared when it comes to harvesting.

Using tools for harvesting certain crops will protect them from damage. I can be a lazy so-and-so, and will regularly try to pull carrots out by hand, forcing the root until it breaks in two. An obvious thing, but it took me a long time to give in and grab a trowel. All root veg will be protected by being dug out gently, while using a fork on bigger specimens such as leeks will help prevent snapped veg. Use a pair of scissors or secateurs for clean cuts when harvesting lettuce leaves and vine crops such as cucumbers.

Time of day will have a bearing, too. The best time to harvest is in the morning, before the temperature rises too much. Veg picked during this time won't have lost moisture in the heat because of evaporation, so they don't limp or wilt as quickly. I've noticed this is particularly relevant for leafy greens and salad, as well as rootier crops like carrots and radish.

Make sure you know what you're going to do with your veg by having a harvesting tactic for each crop. Some crops that are easy to deal with, like beans and winter greens, can just be picked and sorted out but others need a little planning. Onions and garlic must be dry before storage, so make sure you harvest when the weather is good so the crops can be laid out in the sun for a couple of days. A big squash harvest is very heavy, so have somewhere ready to store them, or your car available to take them home. Harvesting can also take longer than you might think, so set plenty of time aside. Harvesting is incredibly satisfying and worth spending some time over, so don't rush. Try to avoid the temptation to leave your harvest on the kitchen top and relax with a cup of tea or kick back in a hot bath. As inviting as this is, deal with your harvest before you do anything else. Crops left out rapidly lose their freshness – unless you are drying them out, get them out of the sun and into the fridge quickly, even if this means not cleaning the dirt off first.

Above all, learn your fruit and veg – underripe or overripe crops do not have as good a flavour as they could have. Knowing what veg is better when young and tender, which should be left to sweeten in a frost and what should be left on the plant to ripen in the sun is all part of enjoying the best tasting, freshest homegrown food. Spotting the optimum harvesting time will come with experience, but here are a few tips for harvesting the most common allotment crops.

Beetroot	Harvest when the size of a tennis ball. Beets will sit in the ground and wait patiently to be picked, but don't let them get too big or they will become woody.
Brussels sprouts	For maximum flavour, harvest sprouts when they are still small (smaller than you would find in the shops). Start harvesting from the bottom, and pull off the dead, yellowy leaves as you go.
Carrots	Watch out for the very top of the carrot poking through the soil. Harvest when they're 3–4 mm (about a tenth of an inch) above the surface. Don't leave them too late as they'll split.
Cavolo Nero and Kale	Pick the leaves just above where the stem meets the plant when they are a deep green colour. About 10–13 cm (4–5 in) is perfect for a kale leaf, while cavolo nero can be a bit longer. Harvest regularly to allow for new shoots to come through, but try to vary the plants you pick from so they all get ample time to recover. Sweetness and flavour are greatly improved if harvesting is left until after the first decent frost of the winter.

Chard and Perpetual Spinach	Chard is a cut-and-come-again plant so responds well to regular harvesting. Again, cut the leaves off where the stem meets the main plant. 15 cm (6 in) is a nice size for a chard leaf.
Courgettes	Check courgette plants every day – turn your back for a minute and you'll end up with marrows! Courgettes are ready when about 15 cm (6 in) long, although they can be harvested smaller.
Cucumbers (outdoor)	Pick outdoor cucumbers when they are about half the length of the conventional ones you find in the shops. Regular harvesting also diverts energy to other cues on the plant.
French beans	It is a fine line between a tender and a tough French bean. Try to harvest before the seeds in the pods become distinct, as this is when the bean will be at its sweetest. Visit the plant as regularly as possible to keep on top of the heavy cropping.
Leeks	You can leave leeks in the ground all through winter, and pick them as and when you need. They're very hardy, so there is no need to dig up your leeks early if you don't want to. When you harvest a leek, make sure you use a spade and dig around the root. Don't be tempted to yank the leek up by the shank as they root pretty solidly and you can easily pull the bottom off. Wash thoroughly as grit gets into the top layers.
Onions and Garlic	Red and white onions and garlic are ready to pull when the stalks die off and bend over.
Parsnips	Parsnips are sweetened by the first frost, so harvest after this for the best taste.

Peas	You can tell if a pea is definitely ready to harvest if you shake the pod and hear the peas rattling inside.
Potatoes	When the potato leaves turn yellow, the crop will stop growing. The potatoes will sit in the ground without complaint until the soil becomes soggy. Get them out before then so they don't rot. Make sure they are dry before storing in paper bags in a cool, dark place.
Purple Sprouting Broccoli	Pick flower shoots or mini florets just before the flower buds open.
Runner Beans	Like French beans, try to pick the pods young, before the seeds are visible. About 20 cm (8 in) is a good size. Left to grow much bigger they'll start to become stringy.
Strawberries	Pick the fruits when they are bright red all over. Strawberries ripen fast, so try to check every day. You don't want to miss the best ones! The hottest part of the day is the best time to harvest strawberries, as the flavour is much stronger when the fruits are warm. Strawberries really do taste incredible straight from the plant, so eat your pickings as soon as you can.
Sweetcorn	Look out for the husks turning brown. Then pull back the husks and make a small incision into the kernel. If the corn is ripe, milky juice will squirt out. If the juice is clear, the corn is still unripe.
Tomatoes	Don't be tempted to pick a pale tomato – you're missing out! Try to leave the fruit on the plant until fully reddened. This way, you'll guarantee your tomato will be as tasty and juicy as possible.

Storing Crops

For the best taste, crops need to be eaten bang on ripeness and many crops deteriorate fast following harvest. However, that doesn't mean that gluts should be wasted, especially at the end of the season. Root crops, potatoes and squashes all keep well for some time after harvest and if you're growing to save money, are vital supplements to true winter crops. Squashes will keep until spring in the right conditions, providing an excellent and versatile source of free food when harvests are scarce.

Before storing crops, leave them out in the dry so that the skin is not wet as this damp will spoil not only the individual vegetable, but potentially the whole crop. Don't wash the skins down before storing either, as this can also bring on rotting and spoiling from the moisture. Darkness and good ventilation is essential to help keep crops dry and free from spoiling – a cupboard under the stairs is perfect, but I have also stored successfully in sheds. Just keep a watch on the temperature so that crops don't get too hot or freeze in very cold conditions. Check regularly for rotting crops, especially if plants are touching each other or are stored in a bag. One rotten specimen can quickly spread the rot and destroy a whole harvest. If you're storing crops in bags, remember to dig as deep as you can to check! Finding a rotting potato at the bottom of the bag can be an unpleasant surprise, but removing decaying spuds quickly is vital to the long-term storage of the crop. Carrots, beetroots, parsnips and other root crops can be stored in boxes within layers of sand. Again, keep these in a cool, dark place such as a shed.

Freezing Crops

Freezing summer veg for eating during the winter is another good way of adding variety to your diet. Like overwinter storing, freezing is a good money-saver as well, as out-of-season veg is expensive to buy in the shops. I often grow late rows of green beans and mangetout purely for freezing to eat later in the year as these veg freeze well, and can be sown in July for later summer or early autumn harvesting and freezing. For the best taste from frozen greens, choose young, fresh veg when freezing. Old, larger crops will be tougher and give a disappointing taste. Many plot holders will blanche their veg before freezing, and although this isn't completely necessary the process does destroy the enzymes that cause ripening, helps to remove dirt and bacteria, and reduces the speed with which vitamins and minerals are lost. Blanching is easy, and simply involves plunging the vegetables into boiling water for about two minutes. When the time is up, drain the veg and cool it in cold water before freezing. Freezer bags are best for storing your veg as they are convenient and you can cram plenty into a small space. Don't overfill the bags and squeeze out any air before tying up and sealing. Freezing in small portions is best, as you can then adapt the amount you use to the number of people you're cooking for. Tightly sealed plastic containers work well too, and can be neatly stacked in a freezer. I use plastic takeaway-type containers to freeze my stewed fruit.

CHAPTER 9

The Allotment Year

Every year, without fail, I find myself marching into my house and making overblown *brrrring* noises, before declaring that 'winter is definitely here'. Normally this is around the beginning of November, when temperatures suddenly dip sharply, and I strengthen the declaration by retrieving my 'winter coat' from its summer break under the stairs. The same applies around my birthday in May, when the first warm day sees me sporting shorts and telling anyone that will listen how 'summer is here'. Of course, to the trained brain, November is about as winter as May is summer, and actually November is autumn, and May is spring. The changing of the seasons may be fairly trivial to most, but they are significant to an allotment holder or vegetable grower as each season triggers key shifts in the environment, and represents times in which different tasks need to be done. Timing is absolutely pivotal to a successful plot, whether it is sowing seeds, fighting pests or harvesting produce, and the seasons spin all around these jobs. Knowing the seasons and all their little growing indicators will help a grower dramatically and provide a routine to work by.

The changing seasons underpin allotment life, and with them bring joy, frustration and an appreciation that we need the rough to give us the smooth. The one thing that running an allotment has taught me above all else is to love the seasons. Each shift into a new season gives me a real hit of energy, and a fresh impetus to keep ploughing on. I love the winter greens as much as the summer tomatoes, and the spring rhubarb as much as the autumn raspberries. The seasons give a purpose to life, and fresh starts just when they're needed.

This chapter is more of a refresher on those important seasonal jobs rather than a detailed framework, but hopefully it'll provide useful little reminders for life on a veg plot during the allotment year. We'll start in spring, when the clocks change, seeds get sown and the magic begins to happen.

Spring

March, April, May

Key Jobs:

- Order seeds
- Clear away winter crops
- Check overwintered plants
- Prepare for strawberries
- Prepare the greenhouse
- Sow seeds
- Chit and plant potatoes
- Watch the weather forecast religiously!
- Control pests
- Think about next year's Hungry Gap

The first walk to our local allotments at the beginning of spring is a wonderful one. On approaching the gate the first thing you notice is the writing on the blackboard outside the allotment shop has been rubbed out and

155

the 'GATE SHUTS 4PM' message replaced with a new communication, telling plot holders that they now shut at 6.30 p.m. I love seeing that sign; it never ceases to make me smile. Confirmation via the allotment committee that the days are drawing out and the busiest period of the allotment year is upon us. Time to get cracking.

Order Seeds

Early spring is the time that pretty much all of us buy our seeds, so if you're planning on purchasing your packets from the allotment shop or local nursery, get in quick as the popular varieties can sell out quickly. There's nothing more frustrating than having to wait for new stock to arrive and consequently delaying your sowing dates. Of course, there is also the internet, with endless seed stockists offering vast ranges of varieties at different prices but again, get your order in sharpish and if you're in a rush remember you'll be waiting a couple of days for delivery.

Clear Away Winter Crops

Before the fun of spring seed-sowing can begin, there are hangovers from winter to deal with. Winter greens, such as kale, chard and Brussels will be dying off and will need pulling up and composting down. Harvest what remains and eat up as soon as you can. Leeks can be left in the ground until the tops go to seed if you've got the space, but if you do find yourself with a glut to use up, leek and potato soup is a sure-fire winner and can be frozen to enjoy at a later date.

The area that your winter crops occupied will need to be cleared and readied for spring and summer planting, so dig in some soil replenisher such as manure or compost, and set aside for later in the year. Try to avoid sowing and planting early crops in this space so that the manure can sink in and the soil recover.

Check Overwintered Plants

Overwintered spring plants such as broad beans, onions and peas will start to perk up with the change in temperature and longer days, but give them a check over, too. Take off any protective cloches and support broad beans by tying them to bamboo canes if they're on the wonk. For an extra energy boost, spread a mulch of compost around the base of the plants.

If you didn't overwinter, sow peas and broad beans either in situ or in pots ready for transplanting later. If the soil is still too cold in early spring, sow in pots or try a length of old guttering and slide out the entire contents into a small trench when things warm up. A good sign of soil warm enough for sowing is the presence of growing weeds. Spread black tarpaulin or fabric over the soil in early spring to attract and hold heat, and warm the soil up quicker.

Prepare for Strawberries

If you need to bulk up your strawberry bed with extra plants, you can still put them in during spring, although they won't produce as well as the established plants. Water regularly, especially once the plants start to flower, and spread straw around the bed. This benefits your strawberry harvest threefold. The straw helps keeps the weeds down (hand pull any weeds that do come out, as strawberry roots are shallow and easily disturbed), and also stops fruit rotting on damp soil after rain showers. I've also found that the rough texture of the straw helps keep the slugs and snails away.

Prepare the Greenhouse

The greenhouse is a super place to dodge those potent April showers, and working in a greenhouse while it rains outside is a real pleasure of spring. Sheltering inside also presents the opportunity to tidy and clean up your pots, canes and tools ready for sowing. Start by removing as much as you can from the greenhouse so you can search all over for any slimies that have taken shelter inside, or anything that could cause disease. Greenhouses are notorious for harbouring pests, especially given all the pots and associated paraphernalia that are normally stored there. Snails and slugs love hiding under these sorts of things, so don't leave any nook or cranny unturned! Get rid of any dead leaves as disease can easily spread around a greenhouse due to the humid conditions and enclosed space.

Give the greenhouse panes a good wash down with hot, soapy water, as poor light can prevent plant growth, while fresh, clear panes brighten the place up no end. Check each pane carefully for breaks or cracks in the grass. Panes of greenhouse glass are often thin, and can easily become brittle from the cold or smash in windy weather. Not only is this dangerous, it can leave holes for pest and vermin to get inside, as well as cold draughts. If you do find a broken pane, local glass companies can cut replacements cheaply for you if you provide measurements.

If you're fortunate enough to have a greenhouse, you will be able to use it to sow seeds earlier than you would outside. The introduction of a greenhouse into my veg-growing life was a revelation and something that added lots of extra enjoyment. It was a learning curve at first, adapting to a new microclimate and higher temperatures, but I wouldn't be without one now. The option to increase the length of the growing season is great for those looking to maximize yields and harvest for longer, as well as for those wanting to try trickier, heat-loving crops such as melons and aubergines. Make sure you keep an eye on the temperature as in a greenhouse it can easily reach 30°C (86°F) even during April, damaging tender seedlings and bringing on too fast other veg that prefer milder conditions. Remembering to open the door in the mornings will help regulate the heat, and moving plants that like cooler temperatures outside during the day will keep them healthy and slow down their growing haste. Some greenhouses have self-opening hatches, and if the heat is something that really becomes a problem, temporary shading paint is also available. A thermometer is a useful thing to keep in any greenhouse, especially for working out whether the temperature is right for germination.

Sow Seeds

Spring is when it all happens for seed sowing, but remember to read the seed packets and stagger sowing according to not only when you want to harvest, but with temperatures in mind, too. Sow salad crops such as spinach, radish and cut-and-come-again leaves early spring in the greenhouse borders or in containers. Early carrot varieties such as Parmex are also worth sowing in the greenhouse in late February or early March, if you've got the space. As the weather warms up later in spring, begin to phase in more tender plants, finishing with tomatoes, courgettes and squashes from mid- to late spring.

Chit and Plant Potatoes

Many growers choose to 'chit' their potatoes before planting out, which involves leaving the spuds out of their bags in the light so that they can sprout. The theory is that a potato will not do much while the soil temperature is below 10 degrees or so, and if left to their own devices the soil won't warm up sufficiently for a potato to sprout early enough. As a result, you're unlikely to get a crop until autumn. An easy way to chit spuds is to pop them into old egg boxes and leave them somewhere warmish, like a conservatory or windowsill.

Organize your potatoes into maincrop and earlies and plant out as soon as you can, remembering to earth up over the top of the plant as it comes through.

Watch the Weather Forecast Religiously!

Become well acquainted with your preferred weather forecaster all through spring, as frosts can occur at any time, and like slugs and snails, are crop killers. Tender plants such as tomatoes, squashes, courgettes, cucumbers and runner beans are particularly susceptible, so don't be tempted to plant them out until the risk of frost has passed. Equally, don't be tempted by quick-fire sales of these plants at big DIY stores and the like. You won't know how well they've been hardened off (if at all) and they often go out on sale far too early in the year when the weather is still too cold for them to survive and flourish. Concentrate instead on growing and nurturing plants of your own that adapt to their home environment. This is the best way of ensuring good, strong crops.

When frost is forecast, move pots inside and huddle them together for extra warmth. Cover plants with horticultural fleece or bubblewrap for protection. Spring is a time of fluctuating temperatures so remember to take the fleece or wrap off the next morning to ensure that the plants don't overheat or sweat.

Control Pests

Whatever you sow or plant, remember to keep an eye on the local slug and snail population. Spring is prime time for them to attack your early crops so undertake regular checks and protect seedlings wherever you can, especially in wet weather. Put down barriers such as eggshells, beer traps and copper and consider sowing extra seeds to compensate for any crop wipeouts. The annual battle against slimies can be a depressing and heartbreaking one, so having a Plan B up your sleeve is paramount.

Look out for blackfly, too, which will likely start on your broad beans but quickly spread to other plants such as courgettes and runners. Spray off blackfly as it arrives with warm, soapy water before it turns into an infestation. This may take morning and evening sprays for a good few days, but keep at it as the plants will recover and produce if the blackfly is kept in check.

Think About Next Year's Hungry Gap

The Hungry Gap is the period between the end of the winter harvests and the start of the early summer crops, such as purple sprouting broccoli, rhubarb, broad beans and peas. If you're a first-time grower, you won't have any produce to harvest during this period unless you got lucky and took on a well-stocked allotment, so think about how you might bridge this gap the following year. It's never too early to start planning for the future on an allotment! What can you grow that will freeze well or store for a long time?

Could you make use of a greenhouse, or are there special varieties that will help fill the hole, such as the aptly named Hungry Gap curly kale?

Summer

June, July, August

Key Jobs:

- Net brassicas
- Finish planting out
- Stake and sideshoot tomatoes
- Keep weeding
- Water and mulch
- Propagate strawberries
- Harvest and manage gluts
- Sowing for winter: spring greens, chard, pak choi, oriental leaves in greenhouse, French beans for freezing

Summer, the season that all of our hard work comes to fruition and we can enjoy oodles of fresh, homegrown food at breakfast, lunch and dinner ... In fact, sometimes there is a bit too much to enjoy as summer is also the season of gluts, so get ready to exhaust the internet and recipe books for yet something else to do with a courgette!

Summer is also a time of competing priorities. With the better weather come holidays, days out with friends and family, other hobbies and all those things we love to do when the sun shines. Keeping on top of summer allotment jobs can be a big ask, so try and make use of the longer days to do the menial but vital tasks such as weeding and watering. Even just a week of neglect can have disastrous consequences, especially in hot weather. Plants won't take long to dry out, and weeds need no second invitation to colonize a plot at this time of year. Try to talk a friend into looking after your veg if you're going on holiday, or maybe return the favour for a fellow plot holder.

Net Brassicas

Get cracking netting any brassica plants if you haven't done so already. Cabbage white butterflies will be preparing to lay eggs and the earlier your plants are protected, the better. Like most pests, the caterpillars will plough through a whole crop in a day or two and what's more the butterflies are determined little critters. Netting will need to be well pegged down, with no hint of access. Keep the nets on until winter to be safe – cabbage white butterflies can hang around into autumn.

Finish Planting Out

Plant late-sown, tender plants such as squashes, courgettes and tomatoes in sunken recesses with a spadeful of organic matter. When watered, the moisture will stay in around the base of the plant rather than run off the hard, sun-soaked ground. Poke a tall stick in next to larger plants so that you know where the roots are. Squashes and outdoor cucumbers trail and courgettes grow very big, so knowing where they are actually planted helps no end when watering. If you're behind, have suffered plant losses or simply forgot to sow something important, plug plants can still be bought. Some nurseries will have stock, otherwise head for the seed companies on the internet. At this time of the year the plants may be expensive but the return on squashes and courgettes will easily outweigh the expenditure.

Stake and Sideshoot Tomatoes

A fully laden tomato plant can be really heavy, so tie the main stem to a bamboo cane for support and keep tying further up as the plant grows. Be careful not to tie the string too tight, though, as it will dig into the stem. Another important summer job to remember is sideshooting – pinching out those extra shoots so that the plant's energy is concentrated on producing tomatoes. This also prevents the plant from getting too bushy and shading the fruit from ripening in the sun.

Keep Weeding

Unfortunately, we'll never beat the weeds. They're indestructible, fit to survive a nuclear winter, and as long as the sun is coming up, the weeds will be the bane of an allotment holder's life. Annoyingly, they all need pulling up, one horrible little weed at a time. Weeding is a rotten job, but during summer they can take over a plot in no time at all. Even a week without weeding is a long enough period for weeds to outweigh crops and there is nothing more disheartening than leaving the plot for a break mid-summer and coming back to a jungle. You'll end up spending a whole day weeding when you could be enjoying the weather and doing other fun stuff. Removing the whole root is really important as snipping off the top won't necessarily kill the weed, and some weeds can regrow from bits of root left in the ground, so do your best to get the whole thing out. This is a lot easier when the weeds are small and yet to establish their root, so little and often before the weed grows to a decent size is by far the best approach. Make use of your hoe to flick the weeds out, and if you come across anything with a big old taproot, get the whole thing out with a spade. Weeds will be competing with your plants for water and nutrients, so the clearer the plot the better. Oh, and learn your weeds from your crops. When veg plants and weeds are at the seedling stage, it can be difficult to tell which is which. My lovely wife made this mistake when weeding carrots. (Angry? Of course I wasn't … honest!) The more expensive seed packets will have a photo of the seedling, so keep them handy for when you need to weed your row. The good news is that during summer you can save time by removing the weeds and leaving them lying where you pulled them. The hot summer sun will kill them off in no time at all.

Water and Mulch

Draw up a rough plan for watering, deciding what plants you are going to water and when, and then stick to it. Plants enjoy consistent watering, especially through the dry summer periods when it might not rain for a fortnight, which makes your watering crucial. As a rough rule of thumb, concentrate on watering hungry plants such as tomatoes, squashes and cucumbers every other day, and hardier, less fussy crops like French beans and winter kale one or two times a week. Seedlings need regular watering while they establish and containers require watering daily during summer as they will dry out rapidly.

Consider installing a water butt to reduce the amount of water you consume from the main supply, especially if the summer is particularly dry. Plants prefer rainwater to water from a tap, so you're doing them a favour as well as the environment. If you don't have a shed to run guttering into a butt, see if you can find an old bathtub to collect rainwater instead. They're not particularly attractive, but they soon fill up and it means that you don't have to keep walking to and from the nearest allotment tap.

Mulching around plants will retain moisture around

them, as well as providing some nutrients and suppressing weeds. Good mulches include compost, manure and leaf mould. I have also used seaweed with success, as well as spent hops. Hops are more readily available now with the increased popularity of microbreweries, and my local brewery leaves spent hops outside in bags for gardeners to take away.

Propagate Strawberries

Strawberry plants shoot out self-rooting runners in mid-summer, which can be potted up and used to increase the size of your beds and replace old plants for free. It's one of my favourite jobs to do, and an easy one, too. I love making this gentle intervention in the strawbs' unfussy bed-spreading process. If I could equate this job to a feeling, it'd definitely be a cheery one. The roots look like little pincers, and will likely be resting on the surface of the soil waiting to get a grip and establish themselves. Once you've found a strong root, pot it up in a small pot of multipurpose compost, pushing the roots a few centimetres under if you can. Lay a stone on the plant to keep it in place, and then

leave it be in a sunny spot to take root. To be safe, I leave the plant a couple of weeks, and give it plenty of water. Once I'm happy that the baby plant is happy, I'll snip it free from the runner with secateurs or scissors. You can check that the plant is rooted by giving it a very gentle tug upwards. If there is resistance, it has rooted. Set aside for planting later in the year.

Harvest and Manage Gluts

Don't overlook regular harvesting as a job on an allotment, especially in the summer. Harvesting needs to be prioritized as a main task as it can affect different plants in different ways. Cut-and-come-again salads and brassicas require harvesting to keep cropping, courgettes need picking before they turn into less tasty and less useful marrows, while tomatoes not only taste better when harvested at the right time but this also helps concentrate the plant's energies into bringing on the younger fruits.

Gluts are unavoidable in summer, especially with high-cropping vegetables like strawberries, courgettes, French and runner beans. Have a plan for crops that go bad quickly, such as freezing or preserving. Chutney is a popular way of preserving tomatoes and runner beans, and soft fruits like strawberries, plums and gooseberries make excellent jam, but don't get caught short for jars! Get any bags or boxes cleaned up and ready for storing potatoes and squashes in good time, and clear room in the shed in anticipation of your harvest.

If possible, keep a record of how many plants you grew, as that will help you decide how many you need to grow to find that balance between feeding the family and drowning under the weight of another basket of runner beans.

Sowing for Winter

There are still seeds that can be sown in mid-summer to provide a crop before winter, or to freeze and use later. Ever year, I sow a couple of rows of French beans between late July and mid-August, specifically to be bagged up and frozen. French beans are so prolific that keeping up with the harvests takes some doing, so it makes sense to freeze for winter. Chard sown during summer will grow quickly and then last all through winter, and spring greens sown every couple of weeks from mid-summer will provide a staggered harvest between January and March. Sow hardy oriental salads direct for salad leaves in winter – mibuna and mizuna are the best varieties.

Autumn

September, October, November

Autumn's a funny season. There are some beautiful, warm days which are lapped up with great zeal because at the back of the mind is the knowledge that the temperature will fall off a cliff any day. My attitude to the allotment and harvesting is very much the same, as there is still lots of summer produce to be enjoyed, but with winter on its way, the life of these crops is numbered. There is also the allotment equivalent of chopping wood and servicing the boiler, such as clearing away decaying plants and giving overwintering crops some protection ready for the inclement weather that's waiting just around the corner.

There is a certain tinge of sadness associated with these jobs, but at the same time pride and satisfaction are bubbling away, too. Final harvesting and tidying up for winter provide me with a warm and fuzzy feeling when I look back on what I've grown, and remember how it was used in the kitchen.

The clocks will change, too, and my beds will be covered in rotting manure rather than veg plants, but it's a great feeling knowing you're part of the cycle.

Key Jobs:

- Harvest squashes
- Dig up and store maincrop potatoes
- Use the last of the tomatoes
- Dismantle structures and clear away finished crops
- Prepare hardy plants for winter weather
- Give rhubarb some TLC
- Plant overwintering broad beans, onions, garlic
- Collect leaves for leaf mould
- Clean tools and equipment
- Start digging over
- Plant fruit bushes

Harvest Squashes

With the increased rainfall of autumn, it is important to harvest anything that is in contact with the ground to prevent the crops from rotting. Pick and store any remaining squashes, as by now the plants will be dying and the fruits will not grow any bigger. Remember to let them dry off in the sun or shed before storing. Use up any damaged ones straight away rather than storing. Squashes are incredibly versatile vegetables so there won't be any shortage of culinary options, including curries, risottos, lasagnes, even cakes. Invest in the best vegetable peeler that you can afford, as this makes skinning them much, much easier!

Dig Up and Store Maincrop Potatoes

Heavy rain can also cause problems for potatoes, by waterlogging the ground and rotting the spuds. Like squashes, the plants will be dying off (signified by the yellowing of leaves) and the potatoes will not grow any bigger so there is nothing to gain from leaving them in the ground. Dig gently so as not to fork the potatoes, and leave them to dry out before storing in hessian or paper sacks in a cool, dark place like your shed or under the stairs. Don't wash the potatoes before you store them as that will add moisture to the bag and cause rot.

Use the Last of the Tomatoes

Outdoor tomatoes can last until November, but after then the weather will cause the fruits to deteriorate, so keep picking and using the red ones fresh as much as you can. If you're still faced with too many tomatoes, making chutney is a popular way of using up gluts. There are thousands of simple recipes in books and on the internet, and spending a couple of hours inside on a raining day cooking delicious chutneys is a very relaxing thing to do. You'll need a big preserving pan, though, as some recipes can use a couple of kilos of toms. Making and freezing passata is also an effective way of using up unwanted tomatoes, and can be used as a basis for sauces later on in the year.

One of the main problems with tomatoes at this time of year is the green ones left on the vine. With the decreasing levels of sunlight during autumn, they will struggle to ripen. Bring the green tomatoes inside and leave them on a sunny windowsill with a banana or two in among them. Bananas release gases that bring on ripening in other fruits, especially tomatoes. If you're considering chutneying, there are also lots of recipes for green tomato alternatives, as well as easy-peasy, spicy green tomato salsas.

Dismantle Structures and Clear Away Finished Crops

It's sad to see plants dying off after a bountiful summer, but a neat and tidied allotment in autumn is a satisfying conclusion to the growing season. Pull up and compost down crops as they finish off, and squeeze as much of the veg plant remains into compost bins as you can, chopping up thicker stems with a spade to speed up the composting process. I also like to empty out the new compost that's at the bottom of the bin and shovel it into big plastic bags. The extra heat of being stored in plastic sweats the compost and helps finish off the process. Take a peek at your compost at this point, as the structure may need balancing given that there is a lot of just one thing going in the bin. Add some extra cardboard, old soil from pots or manure to make sure you don't end up with soggy compost.

Dismantle any structures and remove canes and poles for storage before the weather changes. The canes will go brittle and snap if left out too long and they're worth looking after as the cost of decent garden canes does add up. They'll last much longer if given a quick wipe down and stored in a shed.

Prepare Hardy Plants for Winter Weather

Winter plants are strong old things, but everyone needs a hand in the cold and these chaps are no exception. Check over leeks for rust and discard any that cause concern, and stake tall Brussels and kale to hold them up in strong winds. Get any fleece, bubblewrap or cloches ready to protect plants should heavy snow be forecast, and pull off old, large leaves from the kale and chard to give new shoots the chance to grow on.

Give Rhubarb Some TLC

Once the rhubarb leaves have died away naturally, cut the old stalks down to the ground and apply a hefty mulch of well-rotted manure (the blacker the better). Rhubarb is a pretty hungry plant, and this will aid annual recovery no end and invigorate the crowns for the next year. I scatter two or three spadefuls of manure around the crowns, which helps keep the weeds down as well as nourishing the plant. Try not to completely cover the crown, though, as the manure will keep moisture in and may cause rot. Rhubarb likes to be exposed to some cold during the winter, so make sure you leave any buds poking up above the manure.

Plant Overwintering Broad Beans, Onions, Garlic

If you're planning to overwinter broad beans, onions or garlic, October and November is the perfect time to get them sown and planted. The soil is still fairly warm, so seeds and bulbs will not only germinate but will also establish decent root systems before the winter arrives. Broad bean seeds sown direct in November can take up to a month to germinate, depending on where you are in the country, so don't panic if nothing happens straight away. You can also sow in pots in the greenhouse ready for planting out in spring. This won't necessarily quicken the germination but does mean that they are better protected from the elements than plants standing outside.

Buy onions and garlic in sets and plant in rows. Check regularly after planting in case any hungry birds have helped themselves to the bulbs.

Collect Leaves for Leaf Mould

With leaves falling off the trees left, right and centre, autumn is the time to bag them up and make leaf mould. Leaf mould is super for using as a soil improver, mulch and as part of a homemade potting mix. It's really easy to make, too: bag up the leaves, tie the neck loosely and make a few splits in the bag. Leave for a year or so, and hey presto, leaf mould!

Clean Tools and Equipment

Give any tools a decent scrub down with a wet rag and leave to dry in a warm place, like a utility room. This will prevent rust and prolong the life of the tool. Don't forget all your other plot paraphernalia like pots, boxes, dibbers, string, etc. Washing down pots and seed trays is particularly important as they can harbour pests and disease. Get everything stored away as quickly as possible so the weather doesn't deteriorate them.

Start Digging Over

Rough dig any empty beds before the rain makes the soil too heavy to work. All you need to do at this point is loosen the soil by turning it over, and then add a layer of manure onto the surface. The manure will protect the soil from weather, and gradually break down in time for properly digging in nearer to spring. For double protection, try laying cardboard down in between the soil and manure. The cardboard will rot down with the manure, ready to be dug in later on. If the digging feels like hard work, take plenty of breaks and adopt a little and often approach to stop the job becoming a chore. Know when to call it a day. Don't stay on the plot if you don't want to be there. If you yawn, go home and put your feet up!

Plant Fruit Bushes

The optimum time for planting fruit bushes is the dormant period between November and February, when essentially they're hibernating and no growth occurs. However, November is favourable as the soil is still warm from summer. Bushes are generally available in bare-root or container-grown forms. The main advantage of a container-grown plant is that they can be planted at most times of the year, and can sit in their pots for several weeks before going into the ground. Bare-root bushes are cheaper and, having been grown in a field at the nursery, they do not use as many resources as container plants. They'll arrive freshly lifted and with no soil around the roots. If you choose bare-root plants, try to be prepared. They will need to go into the ground as quickly as possible, but if life gets in the way the plants will be okay in the packaging for a week or so.

When planting a bush, I dig a hole big enough to take the root of the plant and add a decent spadeful of organic matter such as compost or manure. There will be an original soil mark on the bush – try not to plant it deeper than this mark. Water in and then sprinkle a mulch around the base.

Winter

December, January, February

For many, winter is a time to batten down the hatches. I include myself firmly in this camp, enjoying time away from the plot to recharge my batteries and refresh my enthusiasm. I'll spend the majority of my allotment time doing indoor jobs, interspersed with short plot visits for harvesting and some digging when the weather allows.

When it's raining and cold, I'd much rather be cooking up a hearty soup or planning next year's growing schedules!

Key Jobs:

- Enjoy doing nothing
- Continue digging
- Check stored crops
- Check over tools
- New Year's resolutions
- Study plot for frost pockets
- Draw up plot plans
- Browse seed catalogues
- Stock-check seeds
- Continue harvesting winter crops
- Consider early sowings

Enjoy Doing Nothing

Running an allotment is wonderful but it's a commitment, and I've found that come November, the opportunity to kick back and take some time out is most welcome. For me, early winter is a period for the veg grower to chill out, knowing that everything will tick along for a few weeks without much complaint. My parsnips are content to sit in the ground and the onions are planted and sprouting, for example. There are always jobs to do on a plot and loads to do over the winter, but it's also beneficial to enjoy some time away from the plot; for reflection and to recharge batteries. Too much of a good thing and all that.

Continue Digging

Dig beds when you can, but remember, if there has been a prolonged period of rain then the soil is likely to be unworkable. I used to traditionally do a big chunk of my digging during the Chrimbo break but the ground can be heavy by that time, especially in clay areas. Now I try to get most done during early winter before the rain really sets in, and finish off during settled periods. Remember, you only need to rough dig – the important thing is to break up the soil and get some manure on top.

Check Stored Crops

Poor weather presents an opportunity to spend time in the shed checking stored crops, like squashes, apples and potatoes. This is a vital job, though, as removing anything that is beginning to deteriorate or go soft will help stop decay from spreading. You'd best get hardened to grabbing squishy veg, though!

Check Over Tools

Another good indoor job for winter is checking over and repairing any tools that you haven't got around to yet. Clean them down, replace or repair any loose heads and make sure there are none you've accidentally left out on the plot. (If I had a pound for every time I'd mislaid my all-important trowel I'd never have to pay allotment rent again ...) Consider replacing anything that is becoming too broken to use, and being the festive period, you might want to ask Santa for a few new additions.

New Year's Resolutions

The turn of a new year always feels like a milestone in winter. For me, it's time for planning and after a couple of months of downtime and reflection, the new year is the perfect time to make some targets and identify the odd resolution. What bad habits have you picked up that need rectifying? Should you be putting more effort into summer watering? Are you lazy with the weeds? Stick an allotment resolution or two in with the day-to-day ones to help make some improvements on the plot. The real challenge is to stick to your resolutions!

Consider setting yourself a challenge, too. Maybe grow a vegetable that you've never tried before, or attempt to grow a certain value of produce during the year. I like to grow something new or something trickier each year. In the past this has included chillies, melons, aubergines and sweet potatoes.

Study Plot for Frost Pockets

Use the frosts of winter to spot frost pockets so that you know where not to grow tender plants the following year. The frosts will also shorten the length of time that you can grow crops in these spaces, so take a look on the morning of a frost to see which areas are most affected. Frost pockets will be located in the lowest part of your plot, as well as behind hedges and fences.

Draw Up Plot Plans

Use the quiet time between winter and spring to draw up a plot plan for the coming growing season. Specialist software that will automatically work out planting patterns and numbers is available on the web, but producing a plan with good old-fashioned pen and paper can be very satisfying, especially in front of the fire over the course of a few cold, wintry nights.

Try and take rough measurements and get the plan to scale if you can, as this will ensure that you can fit everything in, and save you overspending on seeds that you don't have the room for. Don't be over-optimistic on what you can fit in – keep a good space between plants and rows and don't overcrowd or you run the risk of spreading disease and stunting growth.

Browse Seed Catalogues

The internet is jam-packed full of seed retailers, who will all be advertising their seed ranges for the new year over wintertime. As well as the time-honoured favourites, you'll find all manner of brand spanking new varieties to try, from strains of exotic veg bred to cope with milder British climes, to seeds developed to be more resistant to disease. If you prefer to flick through a nice catalogue at your leisure, most companies will have options to request one by post. It's always heartwarming to come home from work to a doormat full of seed catalogues. Find a big, fat pen and get circling those desirable varieties!

Stock-check Seeds

While you're at it, take half an hour to check on what seeds you already have in your tins. A single packet will contain far more seeds than you could ever wish to grow in a year so over time it is likely that you'll build up a stock of seeds. Remind yourself what you have so that you don't waste money by ordering seeds you don't need. Check for out of date seeds, too, and discard any that are well past their sow-by date. If you've got time, try putting the seeds into sowing order to help remind you what needs sowing when in spring. The very organized among us will label and divide their seed tins, which is a very neat and tidy way to see in the new sowing season.

Continue Harvesting Winter Crops

Hardy cut-and-come-again brassicas like kale and chard will be harvestable all winter if some care is taken to keep them in good condition. Winter produce is sparse and you'll find yourself relying heavily on these veg, so mix up harvests to give each plant a break and encourage healthy regeneration. Keep digging up leeks as and when required, but don't be tempted to pull out any small ones. These will survive the winter and experience a growth spurt in spring, providing a handy harvest during the Hungry Gap. Brussels sprouts will last until the new year, while carrots and parsnips can sit in the ground unless the soil becomes very waterlogged. Early varieties of purple sprouting broccoli can be ready from December, but targeting January and February for harvest brings a welcome change from leafy brassicas.

Consider Early Sowings

As winter draws to a close, attention will turn to seeds that can be sown early, especially if you have a greenhouse and daylight hours hit the ten-hour mark. You may have overwintered broad beans, but if not, seeds can be sown in January or February under glass, along with peas, salad, radishes and early carrot varieties. After the bleak days of winter, even the smallest of sowings brings a wonderful feeling for the gardener, as the cycle of the growing season starts all over again.

CHAPTER 10

There's Always Next Year

Hey Will,

How's things?

I've heard a whisper that you're thinking of jacking in your allotment already. I'm writing to try and talk you out of it.

It's been a rubbish year. Really rubbish. I'd hate to have been a beginner this year. I wanted to write and say that growing your own is not always like this. It's actually normally the opposite.

In a normal year, tomatoes don't get blight. Potatoes don't rot in the sodden ground. Courgettes are the easiest, most productive veg you could ask for. Chillies ripen. Carrots germinate. Squashes don't split ...

One thing I'm sure you know already, is that that thing called the sun also comes out more. The temperature is warmer. The climate is not ridiculously warm in spring, and cold and wet during the summer. Y'know, the weather is steady, and allows for measured vegetable growth, rather than unusually early spurts, or no growth at all in the case of some seeds.

See, I'm a fairly average gardener, yet for the last however many years I've successfully fed myself the best food I've ever tasted. I've never had to try much harder than stick a seed in the ground, water a bit, keep the weeds down and in a few weeks you have something awesome to eat.

I know it seems really tough at the moment, but the chances are next year won't be anywhere near as tricky as this one. Anyone can run an allotment, and it's the best thing ever.

This year, I've had rubbish beets (beets are never rubbish!), caulis, courgettes, squashes, cucumbers, runner beans, mangetout, peas, broad beans, garlic and tomatoes. The only stuff that has been fairly decent are leeks, potatoes, strawberries and French beans. Everything else has been average or worse.

Wandering around our plots, chatting to other allotment holders suggests this is pretty standard fare for this year.

So, I guess I'm trying to say it's not just you. We've all been victims of the dodgy weather. However, aside from the tasty produce, the best thing about growing your own is that there is always next year.

Please stick with your allotment. You really won't regret it. Just write this year off, clear up and dump some manure on the beds and get stuck into a seed catalogue. Have the winter off and get going again in spring.

You're a really organized, methodical bloke, so you're bound to be really good at GYO. I bet you your 2013 seed packets that you'll feel completely different this time next year.

Cheers,

Jono.

I wrote this letter via my blog a few years ago, to a chap I knew who had taken on an allotment but was considering giving up the plot after his first year. That year had been particularly difficult for every grower I had spoken to. The weather had conspired against us on several different levels and pretty much everyone at the local allotments had struggled to produce quality harvests. We all grumbled whenever we saw each other, and morale was low. It wasn't just Will who was considering his veg-growing future, either. Several other growers talked of calling it quits and sticking to the shops for their veg supplies.

I never did hear back from Will, and can only assume that he went ahead with his plans and he passed his plot on to another tenant, but writing the letter made me realize that one of the most important aspects of this whole growing your own lark is to learn from the tough times. Essentially, growing your own vegetables is an easy procedure and as my four-year-old says, 'you sow a seed, give it some water and the sunshine makes it grow'. However, sometimes things don't go to plan. Harvests are poor, seeds don't germinate or disease and pests decimate crops. I've learned over the past decade or so that adopting a Buddhist attitude to allotment life is one of the best ways of running a plot. Sometimes you win, and sometimes you lose. But whatever you do, keep plugging away. It is easy to let the bad times defeat us, but these things are definitely sent to test us, and the next year you'll have learned tricks that will help ensure there isn't a repeat of the previous year's woes. If you find yourself in Will's boat, hang in there, buy some new seeds and crack on again, because failures make you ten times the gardener that successes do. Keep reading, keep learning and keep finding new ways to beat the problems. And grow strawberries and tomatoes. Always grow strawberries and tomatoes.

Of course, you could (and most likely will) have a corking first year on your allotment. Most things will grow rather well, and the resulting crops will provide such a buzz that you'll be hooked for evermore. Yes, you might grow too much, the finicky caulis will come to nothing and the slugs will have nobbled a few rows of lettuce, but generally most things will have grown just fine and dandy.

Either of these outcomes will find you asking the same question: what next? How do you build on what you've learned and what savvy investments can you make to improve your haul even further? Consolidating progress in years two and three is another important goal for the grower, and maintaining that feeling of improvement helps keep spirits high.

My second and third seasons saw a number of different tactics and enhancements on my plot, which were all born from that natural pause for reflection that occurs around this time. I learned a great deal in a relatively short period and subsequently I became very eager to develop and invest further. There are all manner of ways in which a grower will assess after the first year or two, from buying new equipment to trying new methods. Here are a few suggestions for thought after your debut growing season.

Invest in Fruit

If you haven't done so already, buying fruit bushes and plants for the allotment is a sure-fire winner. The initial outgoing can be significant so staggering the purchases over the winter months is a good idea, but the return is excellent as fruit is generally low-maintenance and heavy-cropping, as well as being expensive in the shops. Fruit is annual and a one-off purchase, though, so once you've coughed up the dosh, you won't need to again. What's more, propagating extra plants and bushes from your existing stock is easy, either by taking cuttings or potting up new shoots.

Strawberries and raspberries are the obvious choice, and most growers will plant these in their first year. There is every chance that in the second year you'll want to add even more, as they taste so delicious. Expanding to summer-fruiting and autumn-fruiting raspberries will also lengthen the season, with autumn varieties such as Polka and Autumn Bliss cropping into October.

Blackcurrant and gooseberry bushes are also worth considering, especially as both of these fruits freeze well in the likely event of a glut. Gooseberries come in red and green varieties, with the reds being sweet and the greens requiring cooking. Blackcurrants and gooseberries both make splendid jam, as do loganberries. These are tarter raspberries, but grow like blackberries so are useful for providing cover or growing up ugly walls or sheds.

If you're thinking of adding plums, apples, pears or any other tree fruit to your plot, check the allotment rules first. Some committees require permission to be granted before trees can be planted, or ask that smaller, dwarf stock varieties are used instead. Although it may be three to four years before a good return is had, for me a plum or gage tree is a wonderful addition to a plot. I planted a greengage tree on my plot, and enjoyed a glorious first harvest. It took four years from planting to picking, but was well worth the wait and I'm excited knowing that I'm now set for greengages for many years to come.

Take a Look at Cost

Setting up an allotment can set you back a few quid, with rent, tools, seeds, plants and lots of other items all adding up at the end of the year. It is very easy to spend £50 on seeds, particularly if you get caught up in the heady excitement of impulse shopping in nurseries rather than the more detached ways of the web or seed catalogues, and a well-made, heavy-duty spade can easily cost £30. If you're growing to save money or simply don't want your hobby to break the bank, you might want to set some spending limits or look at ways to reduce how much you fork out (no pun intended). Having already made most of the vital outgoings, year two might be an opportunity to consolidate and keep on plugging away safe in the knowledge that this second year won't set you back too much financially.

Conversely, you might wish to loosen the purse strings and look at investing in some luxuries or plot upgrades ...

A Greenhouse

I was fortunate enough to inherit a greenhouse when I moved home, but if I took on a plot or garden without a greenhouse now, installing one would be high on my list of priorities. A greenhouse will easily set you back £200 or more and will probably be the costliest allotment purchase you ever make, but they expand growing options much further, especially where extending the season is concerned. The extra warmth generated in a greenhouse lets you sow much earlier and harvest much later – I make my first greenhouse sowings in February, and am still harvesting tomatoes in late November – which provides a greater variety of produce over a much longer period. Salad, carrots and broad beans can be overwintered in a greenhouse and options are opened up for more exotic fruit and vegetables, such as aubergines, peppers and melons. They are actually an excellent use of space on a plot, too. Once your seedlings are out, you've got more space to grow other veg undercover, so the space doubles up depending on what time of year it is.

A Shed

A shed is another of the most expensive purchases you'll make on a plot. I know plenty who do without one, but as a space for storing paraphernalia, an area for preparation and somewhere to shelter from prevailing weather, a shed is an important part of any allotment. A sturdy 6 × 4 (a shed measuring 6 ft by 4 ft or 1.8 m by 1.2 m) is perfect if kept tidy and organized.

Sheds come made from a number of different materials these days, but the most common is still the good old timber example. Buy the best you can afford, and treat the timber every summer to protect it and preserve the lifespan. This is particularly important as allotments are often on open spaces, and therefore sheds take a battering from the weather. Metal versions are lower maintenance and hardier, but they're not as visually appealing. There's definitely something quaint about a good old-fashioned wooden shed.

With both sheds and greenhouses, remember to budget for cement and breezeblocks to make a sturdy base on which to install the structure.

Tools

By the end of the first year, the chances are you'll have sourced yourself at least a spade, trowel, rake, fork and watering cans (if not all of these). If you were given your tools or bought them second-hand, you might now be thinking of upgrading to something lighter or of better quality, but if you're happy with what you have, the chances are you'll be looking to expand the range of tools at your disposal. Edgers are excellent for keeping tidy and distinctive borders between grass and bed, and also help stop the grass from growing into your soil. Those feeling flush might want to consider a strimmer, which will make controlling the grass around the plot a doddle. Some plots have lots of grass paths, so a lawnmower might also be on your list, but if you do buy expensive additions, you'll need a shed to lock them away or a big boot to cart them back and forth.

Secateurs are useful for pruning fruit bushes and taking cuttings and shears are just the job for maintaining order in unruly corners. Tougher gardening gloves feel much nicer and offer better protection than thin ones and for the ultimate indulgence, you can't beat a lovely harvesting basket or trug.

Expanding Skills and Knowledge

Above all else, development of growing skills and trying new and exciting veg is likely to hold the greatest appeal come the second year and beyond. Veg such as cauliflowers are more difficult than your regular beetroot, but mastering one of these brings huge amounts of satisfaction. It took me a good three years before I nailed a cauliflower, but boy, did I celebrate. All five pounds of my gorgeous florets were treated to a dumping of Cheddar for a luxurious jumbo cauliflower cheese dish. Growing my first cauliflower felt like a landmark in my allotment life and gave me the confidence to try other types and varieties. If I could nail a cauli, I could grow anything!

Since then, I've tried aubergines, sweet potatoes, peppers and romanesco, a stunning cauli variety with beautifully detailed florets. Some were more successful than others, but growing more difficult veg has also taught me to stay determined and not give up if nothing comes of my seedlings. Try, try and try again, and one day they'll come good. Growing veg is an ongoing refinement process, taking tips from people around you and fusing these with your own experiences.

The same refinement will also apply to your growing environment. As you get further into the growing adventure, you'll learn more about the little microclimate that your plot sits within. No allotment site is the same as another, and sometimes details can vary even on the same site. Indeed, the soil structures of two of my allotments were different despite being just a few hundred yards apart.

Specific things will happen at different times of the year, and you'll learn the localized telltale signs of important elements such as best dates for sowing, when the frosts have passed and how to deal with the soil. The range and volume of pests will often contrast, and sometimes you'll be sent a curveball that you never thought of. When I was fighting the slugs and cabbage white butterflies on my plot, I never expected to have to deal with the local Burnham badgers as well!

A Bigger Plot – or Maybe More!

We're back at the beginning. By the phone again. Ready to make The Call. Except this time, it's different. You're a couple of years in. You've nailed this glorious pastime that we call growing your own. You're experienced and you've learned the ropes. The time for more space has come, and you make that call to find out what else is available.

If you've been renting a half-size plot, this will likely mean moving onto a full-size equivalent, or depending on availability, you might want to take on two half-sizers. At my local allotments, the waiting list was fairly short so it is quite common to see plot holders running two plots simultaneously. Some would use a full- or half-size plot purely for their fruit, with veg going on the other plot, while others might make a split between their low-maintenance, space-hungry crops such as potatoes, leeks and onions and the resource-hungry plants like tomatoes and runners. For a time, I did this but used my garden for the plants that need regular care or harvesting, and used an allotment for spuds and other crops that I could harvest and store periodically.

A bigger space opens up a plethora of new opportunities, including a stab at self-sufficiency and the possibility of not needing to buy fruit and veg from the shops again. This is often seen as the holy grail by many growers, but requires a lot of planning and dedication, which should be balanced against what is actually worth spending the time growing. As we've talked about before, putting the effort into a cracking harvest of expensive, long-lasting and brilliantly flexible squashes is likely to be more advantageous and value for money than using some of that space for onions and garlic. Of course, money is not always the driving factor, and reducing food miles or reliability on shops and growing organically might all be reasons for growing your veg. Extra space will let you explore all these ideas, and who knows, you might even follow the dream that many of us carry, and sell up for a cottage in the country and go for the smallholding life!

Whatever you choose to grow, and in whatever volume, I hope that the first year was everything that you dreamed it would be, and as well as eating some delicious homegrown food, you finished with a few quid in your pocket, too. My first year opened up a whole new world in front of me, where I fell in love with food I'd previously never heard of. There are so many different fruits and vegetables I'd have stumbled through life without enjoying if I hadn't have taken on my allotment back in 2007, and sometimes I get a tad jealous of newcomers to the hobby, with all this fun of discovery still ahead of them. But then I remember the best part of growing your own and eating within the seasons: that unbridled joy stays with you – harvests are enduring, and I never fail to get excited at the thought of a fresh one.

An allotment is also your space to do whatever you wish, and be completely and utterly yourself. I can lose hours there, chatting to myself, scratching my head and pondering, completely oblivious to what's going on around me. I don't think I've experienced anywhere else that allows such a switch-off. I've learned that having a special place to be yourself is a less obvious but equally important reason to run an allotment, and this is reflected by the different growing styles, colours and sheds. So many different people in one place, all happy growing and tinkering in their own little worlds.

I've enjoyed an amazing ten years on wonderful allotments and in my garden. I took a plot on, knowing nothing, yet I've fed me, my wife and now my little boys, fresh, delicious fruit and vegetables throughout that time. I've had failures, successes and laughs while saving myself thousands of pounds.

Against the often hectic backdrop of modern life, my allotment is something that has always felt so right and so friendly, and has always been there to give me a lift when I needed one. With my harvests going from the soil to the fridge, to the plate, to my lunchbox and even to my wedding, my allotment runs right through my life, like a best friend. If it were an emoji, it would be a great big smiley face.

Happy growing.

Index